NATIONAL LITERACY TESTS Y9

A+ National Practice Tests graduated difficulty with answers

Lynne Marsh
Wendy Bodey
Virginia Ayliffe
Julie Mitchell

A+ National

National Literacy Tests Year 9
1st Edition
Lynne Marsh
Wendy Bodey
Virginia Ayliffe
Julie Mitchell

Publishing editors: Jana Raus, Jane Moylan
Project manager: Mia Yardley
Senior designer: Ami Sharpe
Text designer: Ami Sharpe
Cover designer: Ami Sharpe
Cover image: Shutterstock
Photo researcher: Libby Henry
Production controller: Alex Ross & Damian Almeida
Reprint: Jess Lovell

Any URLs contained in this publication were checked for currency during the production process. Note, however, that the publisher cannot vouch for the ongoing currency of URLs.

Reprint of ISBN 9780170181761

Acknowledgements
VCE ® is a registered trademark of the VCAA. The VCAA does not endorse or make any warranties regarding this Cengage product. Current and past VCE Study Designs, VCE exams and related content can be accessed directly at www.vcaa.vic.edu.au

We would like to thank the following for permission to reproduce copyright material:
© Australian Human Rights Commission: p. 49; © 2008 ACTNOW (http://www.actnow.com.au/): pp. 46 (text), 50 (text); © 2009 Commonwealth of Australia: p. 88; Corbis Australia: pp. 26 (Uluru), 84; Discovery Channel News (news.discovery.com) © 2009 Discovery Communications, LLC: 86; © Inspire Foundation (http://au.reachout.com/): p. 82 (text); iStockphoto/Terry VanderHeiden: p. 55; Jupiterimages Corporation: pp. 2, 25 (all), 26 (flag), 26 (pie), 26 (wattle), 35 (all), 68 (all), 102 (all); Shutterstock: pp. 46 (image) Anthony Harris, 78 eldirector77, 44 Eric Isselée, 45 ilker canikligil, 47 Yuri Arcurs, 48 (image) Jan Daly, 50 (image) Nicemonkey, 51 Jason Bennee, 53 (image) Morgan Lane Photography, 54 (image) Tania Zbrodko, 80 Mike Von Bergen, 81 michaeljung, 82 (image) Miodrag Gajic, 87 olly, 90 WITTY234.

P 13 © 2000 Used by permission of Educators Publishing Service, Cambridge, MA, 1-800-225-5750, www.epsbooks.com

P 48 (text): Extract from Rollercoaster, 'Can Animals Talk?' written by Hugh Davies and edited by Ivana Rowley, was first published by ABC Online, and is reproduced by permission of the Australian Broadcasting Corporation and ABC Online. (c) 2009 ABC. All rights reserved.

P 54 (text): Extract from BTN 'Energy Drinks' by Kirsty Bennett, first published by ABC Online, 9 September 2008, is reproduced by permission of the Australian Broadcasting Corporation and ABC Online. ©2008 ABC. All rights reserved.

P 83: Extract from RollerCoaster 'The Science of Chocolate' by Heather Catchpole, first published by ABC Online, reproduced by permission of the Australian Broadcasting Corporation and ABC Online. ©2008 ABC. All rights reserved.

Every effort has been made to trace and acknowledge copyright. However, if any infringement has occurred the publishers tender their apologies and invite the copyright holders to contact them.

For product information and technology assistance,
in Australia call **1300 790 853**;
in New Zealand call **0800 449 725**

For permission to use material from this text or product, please email **aust.permissions@cengage.com**

ISBN 978 0 17 046286 0

Cengage Learning Australia
Level 7, 80 Dorcas Street
South Melbourne, Victoria Australia 3205

For learning solutions, visit **cengage.com.au**

Printed in Malaysia by Papercraft.
5 6 7 26 25

Detailed information

Introduction

Literacy and numeracy are the fundamental building blocks of learning in any subject. Knowing what you can do and where you need to improve is vital for all Australian students, teachers and parents. The NAPLAN* (National Assessment Program – Literacy and Numeracy) tests in literacy and numeracy help governments find out how Australian students are progressing and help to identify what you know and what you don't know. The results of the tests also help you and your teachers plan what you need to learn next.

Tests can sometimes be a little daunting; however, there are practical steps you can take to ensure you will successfully sit a test. You will be best prepared for any test when you understand what is being tested, how you will be tested, and when you are mentally and physically prepared for the test. This book provides practical advice and strategies to ensure that you are test ready and contains practice tests so you can see what to expect in the tests.

This book and the accompanying NelsonNet website provide:

- ✔ **Test tips:** advice on how to successfully sit tests, information about what is tested and how it is tested, hints on responding to different question types and how to act on your results.
- ✔ **Key skills:** summary information about each of the three Literacy tests: Reading, Language Conventions and Writing. This includes important information about what each of the tests cover including the skills, knowledge and understandings you may be required to demonstrate. You will also find examples of actual student responses demonstrating different levels of understanding.
- ✔ **Practice question sets:** includes practice question sets for each of spelling, punctuation, grammar, reading and writing. These tests are designed so that you can build your skills and confidence during the first part of the year leading up to the test.
- ✔ **Two full-length practice tests:** two full-length detachable tests for each of Language Conventions (spelling, grammar and punctuation), Reading and Writing. One paper is for you to use as a practice test, and the other is for you to hand in to your teacher. These tests follow the format of the NAPLAN* tests and are the level of difficulty you can expect to find when you sit the actual tests. These are ideal for practice during the month leading up to the test.
- ✔ **Answers:** for easy reference, answers to all workbook questions can be found on NelsonNet, https://www.nelsonnet.com.au/free-resources.
- ✔ **Useful icons:** icons are used throughout the resources to help you quickly find other important information in the resources and support your understanding.

Hot tips: keep one step ahead by heeding these hot tips. The tips often relate to things many students forget to do or can do better with a little planning.

World Wide Web link: provides a useful link to further information available on the Internet.

* **This book is not an officially endorsed publication of the NAPLAN project and is produced by Cengage Learning independently of Australian governments.**

9780170462860

About the authors

Lynne Marsh

Lynne Marsh is our lead author for both of the Y7 and Y9 books, and joins us with a wealth of teaching and assessment experience from NSW. She has been a co-author of *The Text Book* series, several resources for The English Teachers Association, the NSW Department of Education and Training and is currently teaching in NSW.

Wendy Bodey

Wendy draws on diverse experience gained working at Curriculum Corporation, the Australian Council for Educational Research and as a teacher. Wendy has authored a variety of assessment materials and resources and has played key roles in national and jurisdiction assessment programs including the inaugural National Assessment Program Literacy and Numeracy (NAPLAN) tests.

Virginia Ayliffe

Virginia Ayliffe is a co-author on the renowned *Shakespeare Unplugged* series, which last year won the APA Educational Excellence award for best Secondary Series. She currently teaches at Somerville House in Queensland.

Julie Mitchell

Julie Mitchell has authored and compiled several English texts, and has many years' experience teaching secondary English in Victoria. She has also written curriculum resources in the field of Values Education with Curriculum Corporation. She is now involved in teaching preservice teachers at the University of Melbourne.

Test Tips

Year 9 is a pivotal year in your education. Tests provide an important source of information to assist you and your teacher to review your learning goals and to ensure that you are on track to meet your future aspirations. Follow the practical advice provided throughout the rich resources in this book and you will be prepared to successfully sit the NAPLAN* tests and most tests at the secondary level.

Make literacy your friend

Make sure you are familiar with English language conventions and that you can correctly spell common, difficult and more challenging words. Tackle crosswords and other language puzzles to reinforce and expand your vocabulary. Set yourself a challenge to learn a new word every day to add to your repertoire. Experiment with your writing before the test so that you can get ongoing feedback about how well you express yourself in different genres. Start using new words well before the test so that you can try them out before a test situation. It might be using a word such as 'ubiquitous' rather than 'everywhere'. You need to be confident in your understandings so that you can make the correct word, grammar and punctuation choices. The Language Conventions, Reading and Writing Key Skills sections include important rules, conventions and other information that you will find useful during the tests and to build your knowledge. Refer to the Glossary for an explanation of important words you should know and understand.

Dot your i's and cross your t's

In Literacy tests it is important to make sure the little things are also correct. Avoid making common errors as these may detract from the quality of your answer and impact on the score or mark you get for your answer. One common error students make is overusing apostrophes, for instance adding one whenever a word ends in 's'. It is important you understand the conventions of punctuation use, such as the use of apostrophes, so that you apply punctuation correctly. Consider the following two sentences.

My friend's investments were made during a turbulent period in the economy.

My friends' investments were made during a turbulent period in the economy.

There is only one difference in these two sentences, the position of the apostrophe in the word 'friends'. There is however, a significant difference in the meaning of each sentence. The first sentence is about one friend while the second is about more than one friend. This type of difference in meaning is likely to be important in your answer or response.

Another common error is incorrect word choice. Sometimes this occurs because the word sounds the same (such as 'principle' and 'principal'). Many students confuse the use of such words as 'there' with 'their' and 'they're' and they might similarly confuse 'to' with 'too' and 'two'. Always check that you use the correct word. Some errors are made due to insufficient knowledge of the word meaning and usage. Care needs to be taken to avoid misuse of words as this may introduce a 'clanger' to your answer and detract from what would otherwise be an excellent response.

Ensuring details such as these are correct will enhance the quality of your answer and ensure the marker is not distracted by what might appear to be careless errors in your work. Details do matter, so remember to dot your i's and cross your t's.

Know the type of answer required

The Writing test requires you to write on a set topic. There is quite a difference between an average and an excellent response. Follow the advice provided in these resources, particularly the advice provided in the Writing key skills section. This section includes annotated examples so that you can see how the marking criteria are applied to actual student responses. The Reading and Language Convention test questions cover a range of aspects and difficulty levels and generally the questions become more difficult as you proceed through each test. The Spelling, Grammar, Punctuation and Reading key skills sections include important rules, conventions and other information that you will find useful during the tests and to build your knowledge.

Many of the questions in the Language Conventions test and the majority of those in the Reading test are set out in multiple-choice format. The correct answer is provided along with some other, often attractive, options for you to choose from. You need to identify the correct response.

* **This book is not an officially endorsed publication of the NAPLAN project and is produced by Cengage Learning independently of Australian governments.**

9780170462860

The Reading test questions relate to texts provided in the reading stimulus booklet. A small number of these questions require you to write your answer. These questions usually require you to provide an explanation or evidence from the text to support your answer to the question. Your answer will be marked based on the understanding you demonstrate so it is important your answer is clear and unambiguous.

Multiple-choice questions give you the answer

Multiple-choice questions provide the correct answer along with other incorrect options to choose from. Start by working out the correct answer. If your answer is one of the options provided you will feel reasonably confident that you have correctly answered the question. The best way to check this is to make sure that all the other options are incorrect.

Some students think that if they are not sure of an answer they should stick with a particular guess, for example to always choose 'B' when unsure. This is not a recommended strategy; it is a myth that 'B' or any other option is usually correct. Most tests have a good mix of correct answers for options A, B, C or D that are randomly spread across the test with approximately the same number of As, Bs and the other options available. The best way to proceed when you are not sure which option is the correct answer is to eliminate the incorrect options. The following tip provides specific advice on eliminating incorrect options. In the meantime don't forget that the correct answer is one of the answer options provided – it's just a matter of you correctly identifying it.

Eliminate incorrect options in multiple-choice questions

The options provided in multiple-choice questions are chosen because they are common errors that students make. Therefore you need to think through the options carefully so you are not distracted by attractive, but incorrect, options. Consider the following question:

Which of the following correctly completes the sentence?

If they had needed my help I [ ] stayed there all night.

- ☐ wouldve
- ☐ would've
- ☐ would of
- ☐ would'ave

First eliminate any implausible options. It is easy to eliminate 'wouldve' and 'would'ave' as these are not words in the English language. The remaining two options are 'would've' and 'would of'. You can eliminate 'would of' as this is not the correct contraction – while it sounds like the right contraction, its spelling shows that it is not correct. This leaves the option 'would've'. It is important you check that this remaining option is correct to ensure you have not made any accidental mistakes as you eliminated the other options. The option 'would've' is the correct contraction of 'would have' and is also a correct answer to complete the sentence. You have identified the correct answer.

Use strategies such as these to eliminate options and to also assist you to confirm the correct answer.

Make sure your answers show your understanding

When you answer a question, make sure your answer is clear and unambiguous. Consider the following Reading question and the selection of possible responses. This is an approach you can apply to any question that requires you to demonstrate an understanding of the text.

For this purpose we will imagine you have read the corresponding text, in this case 'Frogs Return'. The text describes the return of frogs to the Wilson Creek area after an absence of 15 years. Scientists regard the presence of frogs in an area as one of the best indicators of a healthy environment. Scientists credit the improvement at Wilson Creek to work by local community groups to restore the area and are pleased the creek can again sustain frog life.

You will then be asked questions about the text, for example:

Why were the scientists excited about the presence of frogs at the creek?

Student One's answer: They are important.

This response is too vague and does not clearly convey why the scientists would be excited about the frogs presence. An answer of this quality would be marked incorrect.

Student Two's answer: Not seen there for years and a sign of good environment.

This answer includes an explanation for the scientist's excitement – the return of frogs and this being evidence of an improvement in the environment. As this answer demonstrates an accurate understanding of the text it is credited as correct.

Remember you will not be penalised for incomplete sentences, or indeed, incorrect spelling, grammar or punctuation. You should, however, ensure your answer is clear and legible so that the marker can understand your response and credit the understanding you have shown.

Be calm and don't panic

On test day make sure you have had a good night's sleep and that you have eaten breakfast so that you are physically prepared to do the test. Be confident in your preparation and you will be ready to tackle the test. Use the pre-test and test day checklists provided to assist your preparation.

It is important that you answer each test question to the best of your ability as this will provide the best guide for your future learning requirements. Tests help to identify your strengths and any potential areas for further development that you may have. It is important that you discuss your results with your teacher to ensure your learning program and goals are the most appropriate for you.

Know your tests

It is good to know as much as you can about the tests so that you have an understanding of what is being tested and how it will be tested. There are three Literacy tests, one for each of Reading, Language Conventions and Writing. Language Conventions incorporates spelling, grammar and punctuation. Understanding more about the types of skills assessed in each test is useful information for you as a test taker. Use the resources provided to find out more about the composition of the tests including the content coverage, the aspects included and the marking criteria used.

The Literacy tests are conducted over three sessions: there is a test for each of Reading, Writing and Language Conventions.

The Reading test requires you to read a selection of texts and answer questions to demonstrate your understanding of each text.

The Writing test requires you to respond to one writing prompt; it may be a narrative writing task or another genre such as a recount or an exposition. Your writing is assessed against specific criteria. See Tip 11 for a link to information about this year's test genre and marking criteria.

The Language Conventions test comprises spelling, grammar and punctuation. You are required to correct spelling errors and identify correct spelling, grammar and punctuation.

Watch the time but don't hurry

The time available to complete each of the tests is adequate for most students to comfortably complete it, so be conscious of the time as you work through the test but don't rush your answers.

You have 40 minutes to complete the Writing task including an allowance of five minutes for planning at the start and five minutes of editing at the end of the session. It is important to plan what you are about to write if you are then to make the most of your 30 minutes writing time. Stick to your plan so that you do not run out of time. Your practice sessions will have prepared you for this well. It is also important you make use of the last five minutes to reread your work and make any necessary corrections. Your test administrator will advise you when you have five minutes left.

In the Reading test you have just over one minute per question and in the Language Conventions test you have just under a minute per question. Start by working through the questions you are most confident to answer and do quick checks as you go. Use the remaining test time to tackle questions you are less sure of. Do not spend too much time on anyone question until you have completed all other questions in the test. Circle question numbers you wish to return to so that you can quickly relocate them.

Have your own watch so that you can monitor the time yourself rather than be dependent on time information at the testing venue.

Prepare well

Some students feel nervous when it comes to test time. The best way to manage this is by ensuring you are well prepared before test day, and then you will have no need for any concern. Find out as much as you can about each test well before you sit them so that you have an understanding of what is being tested, and how it will be tested. Read through the various Key skills sections and the Glossary to revise important facts, rules and other information that you will find useful during the test and in building your knowledge.

Work through the spelling, punctuation, grammar, reading and writing practice sets provided to give you a better sense of what the test will be like and to assist you to identify any areas that you may need to revise. Use these sessions to monitor how well you use your time.

Then complete the two full-length detachable tests incorporating Language Conventions, Reading and Writing. The first is designed for you to use as a practice test, the other to hand in to your teacher. Discuss your test results with your teacher and seek their feedback on how well you performed and any areas you might improve.

Keep up to date with information from your test authority

It is important to keep up with any information about the test. Your test authority will provide regular updates. Contact details for all Australian Test Administration Authorities for the NAPLAN* tests can be found at:

www.naplan.edu.au/test_administration_authorities.html

Other general information about the tests and specific information such as the genre for this year's writing test can be found at:

www.naplan.edu.au/

* **This book is not an officially endorsed publication of the NAPLAN project and is produced by Cengage Learning independently of Australian governments.**

Pre-test checklist

Use this checklist to ensure you are prepared to successfully sit the tests.

	Activity	Main resource
❐	Know the important words and terms used in literacy	Glossary
❐	Be familiar with the keys skills for each test – Reading, Writing, Language Conventions (spelling, grammar and punctuation)	Key Skills
❐	Be familiar with English conventions	Key Skills
❐	Build your skills and knowledge informally too	Read widely Tackle puzzles and games Learn word definitions
❐	Understand the writing marking criteria and how it is applied	Writing marking criteria Writing Key Skills
❐	Complete the practice question sets to get a feel of the tests and questions types	Complete practice set questions for each test
❐	Check your answers against the solutions to evaluate your strengths and any areas you need to revise	Practice question sets solutions for each test
❐	Get advice on tackling the tests	Test tips
❐	Complete Practice test 1, the same length and level of difficulty you can expect in the test	Practice test 1 for each test
❐	Check your answers against the solutions to evaluate your strengths and any areas you need to revise	Practice test 1 solutions
❐	Complete Practice test 2 and hand in to your teacher	Practice test 2 for each test
❐	Ask your teacher for feedback on your performance and use of time	You and your teacher
❐	Keep updated on test information from your assessment authority	Test Administration Authority

9780170462860

Test day checklist

Use this checklist to ensure you are prepared on test day.

Day before the test

	Activity
❐	2B pencils, an eraser and a sharpener ready to take
❐	Have a good night's sleep

Test morning

	Activity
❐	Have breakfast
❐	Take watch, pencils, eraser and sharpener
❐	Arrive at school, or the testing venue, well before the session commences

During the test – Reading and Language Conventions

	Activity
❐	Be confident in your preparation
❐	Monitor your time during the test
❐	Work through the test, completing easy questions first
❐	Read each question carefully, underline important words
❐	Don't spend too much time on any one question
❐	Circle the question number of any question you need to return to
❐	Make sure your written answers are legible and show good understanding
❐	Only write in the box or on the lines provided
❐	Select the correct options in a multiple-choice question; check the other options are incorrect
❐	Choose the correct number of answer options only (usually one) and shade in the box(es) completely.
❐	If you change your answer, rub out the other answer completely
❐	Go back to complete unanswered questions
❐	Check your work, make sure you haven't skipped any questions

During the test – Writing

	Activity
❐	Know the particular genre being tested, for example: narrative, recount
❐	Plan your writing, making a clear connection to the stimulus
❐	Meet genre expectations in your writing
❐	Keep in mind the marking criteria and how it is applied
❐	Only write on the lines provided and within the set length limitations
❐	Be mindful of the time, allow time to check your work
❐	Reread your writing and make any necessary revisions
❐	Check your spelling, grammar and punctuation

After the test

	Activity
❒	Discuss your results with your teacher
❒	Identify your strengths and any potential areas to revise
❒	Consider these results together with other evidence of your progress
❒	Review learning goals to ensure they are appropriate

9780170462860

Key Skills: Language Conventions

In order to communicate with each other we have to agree on a series of codes that we can all understand. Spelling, punctuation and grammar are the codes we use to govern our written and spoken communication. In order to communicate clearly and effectively we follow the conventions (what is expected and accepted) of these codes.

The following demonstrates the problems we can find ourselves in if we don't have a good grasp of our language!

The newly formed Year 9 choir will sing for the first time at tonight's concert and a real threat is anticipated.

Spelling

By the time you reach Year 9 it may be the case that you don't spend lots of time in class focusing on spelling and strategies for achieving accuracy. It's a good idea to remind yourself of practices that you may have been taught in earlier years that can assist you in spelling words, both known and unknown, accurately.

- If you are a visual learner 'Look, Say, Cover, Write, Check' is a great strategy to use. Look at the word, say it to yourself, then cover it up, write it out and then check for accuracy.
- Look for words with the same pattern, such as *could*, *would*, *should*, and learn these as a group. Letter patterns can often help you read words that you're unsure of, or haven't seen before. They are particularly useful because English words are not always spelt the way that they sound. This means we can't always rely on the sounds of letters to help us spell or read; for example *tion* sounds like *shun*.
- Spelling and meaning can be linked. Consider words with related meanings. For example: two, twin, twice (this will help you to remember the w in two).
- Look for words-within-words. For example: football – foot, all, ball.
- Chunk the word – spell the word out in bits and break it up into smaller parts. For example: in – ter – net, tech – no – lo – gy.
- Use memory aids. For example: practice / practise – ice is a noun, so practice is a noun and practise is a verb.
  Stationary / stationery – a car is stationary.
  Piece – a piece of pie.
  Teacher – there is an ACHE in every teacher!!!
- Build word families starting with a base word. For example: bore: boring, boredom, etc.
- Identify the part of the misspelt word with which you are having a problem. Link this with other words you know with the same spelling pattern.

The Language Conventions section will assess your ability to use accurate spelling. The first type of question will ask you to identify the misspelt word and write the correct answer. The second type of question will identify the spelling error for you and ask you to write the answer.

Example type 1:
The first type of question on the test will state:

'Each sentence has one word that is incorrect.

Write the correct spelling of the word in the box.'

The comittee vote on the new president has been delayed again. [ ]

The word that has been misspelt is: **comittee**. In the box, write the correct answer – committee.

Example type 2:
The second type of question will state:

'The spelling mistakes in these texts have been circled.

Write the correct spelling for each circled word in the box.'

Statistics suggest that the form of (diabetis)

[ ] 1

usually associated with adults is much (hire)

[ ] 2

in children than (originaly) thought.

[ ] 3

The correct answer for box 1 is 'diabetes'. The correct answer for box 2 is 'higher'. The correct answer for box 3 is 'originally'.

Punctuation

Another set of codes we use, to ensure that we communicate clearly, is punctuation. There are also conventions that govern the way we use these signs and symbols. If we didn't use these in the accepted way, the following sentence taken from a book by Lynne Truss could be misinterpreted.

The panda eats, shoots and leaves.

If the comma is inserted after 'eats', then the sentence means that after a panda eats his meal, he shoots, perhaps a weapon, and then leaves the scene of the crime. The writer probably doesn't mean this! Without the comma after 'eats', the sentence tells us that pandas eat shoots of plants and leaves.

Consider the following short texts:

i would like to apply for a job with your store for two years i have been employed as a sales assistant at mitchells i sold nothing that i did not take pride in i am sure it will be the same if i work for you

It is extremely difficult to read this piece and establish a clear meaning.

In the next instance it is punctuated:

I would like to apply for a job with your store. For two years I have been employed as a sales assistant at Mitchell's. I sold nothing that I did not take pride in. I am sure it will be the same if I work for you.

The punctuation marks make the meaning clear. However, look what happens when those marks are moved!

I would like to apply for a job with your store for two years. I have been employed. As a sales assistant at Mitchell's I sold nothing. That, I did not take pride in. I am sure it will be the same if I work for you.

The meaning is completely different.

In a university English class the lecturer wrote the following on the board: 'A woman without her man is nothing'. She asked her students to punctuate it correctly.

How many different ways can you punctuate this sentence, and how is the meaning altered?

Punctuation provides the reader with the directions on how to sound out what is written. Let's face it, punctuation really matters!

You should make sure that you know about the correct usage of the following punctuation marks:

- commas
- full stops
- capital letters
- apostrophes
- questions marks
- quotation marks – for direct speech, short quotations, indicating special words or phrases
- exclamation marks
- colons
- semi colons
- dashes
- parentheses (brackets).

The test for Language Conventions will assess your ability to use some of the above punctuation marks by asking you to identify the correctly punctuated sentence. The question will state:

'Which sentence has the correct punctuation?'

You then need to select the sentence which is accurately punctuated and shade one box – the one which corresponds with the accurately punctuated sentence.

You may be asked to choose a response that has no punctuation errors OR shade boxes to indicate where a punctuation mark should go.

NOTE: In all cases you must shade the box which corresponds with the accurate response. If a question asks you to select the correctly punctuated sentence and the punctuation is accurate in more than one response, select the sentence that is accurate in all ways. Perhaps the punctuation is accurate but the use of capital letters is not. Choose the sentence that is correctly punctuated and also uses capital letters accurately.

For example:

1 **Which sentence has the correct punctuation?**

- ☐ **The drought has been severe in New South Wales**
- ☐ **The drought has been severe in New South Wales.**
- ☐ **The drought has been severe in New south wales.**
- ☐ **The drought has been severe in new south wales.**

The best answer is the second as all capital letters are accurate and there is a full stop at the end of the sentence.

The second type of punctuation question will ask you to shade one box to indicate where a particular type of punctuation mark needs to be added.

For example, if there is a missing apostrophe, the question will state:

'Shade one box to show where the missing apostrophe (') should go.'

9780170462860

The teachers job is to help the students understand the demands of the questions.

Shade the box after the 'r' in teachers. This is the correct response because there is one teacher and she owns the job of helping the students understand the demand of the questions.

Grammar

The final convention on which you will be assessed is grammar. Using the conventions of grammar ensures that we express ourselves accurately.

Misplacing a prepositional phrase can be very misleading. For example: 'She could not explain why she wanted to get married to her mother.' The writer does not mean that the girl wanted to get married to her mother! The details in the sentence need to be repositioned. It should say: 'She could not explain to her mother why she wanted to get married'.

The main type of question about grammar will state:

'Which of the following correctly completes the sentence?'

For this question, you will need to shade one box which corresponds to the word that will make the sentence grammatically correct.

Kaz [ ] shopping if she had sufficient money.

- ☐ would not gone
- ☐ will have gone
- ☐ would have gone
- ☐ have gone

To answer the question, shade the correct form of the verb. The correct answer for the space in the sentence is 'would have gone'.

Another type of question you may encounter will have four similar sentences and you will be asked to shade the box which corresponds with the correct sentence. The question will state:

2 'Which sentence is correct?'

- ☐ The argument is between Sam and it.
- ☐ The argument is between Sam and me.
- ☐ The argument is between Sam and myself.
- ☐ The argument is between myself and Sam.

To complete this question, shade the box next to the second sentence. 'The argument is between Sam and me' is correct.

You should make sure that you know about the following aspects of grammatical usage:

- sentence structure – simple, compound and complex sentences
- sentence types – questions, statements, commands and exclamations
- subject-verb agreement
- group composition – verb group, noun group, adjective group and adverb group
- prepositions
- pronouns – subject, object, possessive, reflexive, relative
- conjunctions
- clauses and phrases
- conditionals
- active / passive
- verb tenses.

Key terms: adjective, adverb, apostrophes, commas, complex sentence, conjunctions, conventions, pronouns, punctuation, tense. See the Glossary on page 107 for definitions of these terms.

TEST 1: Language Conventions

Instructions

- A correct answer scores 1 mark, and an incorrect answer scores 0.
- Marks are not deducted for incorrect answers.
- No marks will be given if more than the required number of boxes are shaded (most questions require one answer).
- Choose the alternative which most correctly answers the question and shade in the box next to it.

Spelling

WRITE YOUR OWN ANSWER

Each sentence has one word that is incorrect.
Write the correct spelling of the word in the box.

1 Learning the piano takes a good deal of concerntration.

2 When you're reading a map you need to aurientate it correctly.

3 Many people died of plage in the middle ages.

4 The desperate student offered me an inducment to cheat during the test.

5 The community response to the victims of the bushfires has been holehearted.

6 I recieved a delicious box of chocolates for my birthday.

WRITE YOUR OWN ANSWER

The spelling mistakes in the following text have been circled.
Write the correct spelling for each circled word in the box.

7 When I went for my apointment at the new medical clinic

I was feeling frightfull. I thought that the consultation might

end in hospitalisation. I need not have paniced. My temperature

was quite high but the doctor said that if I were conscientius

about getting good rest it would all be resoulved in a few days.

Punctuation

SHADE ONE BOX

1 Which sentence has the correct punctuation?

- ☐ I asked Hamish, 'Did he ask me to ring back'?
- ☐ I asked Hamish? 'did he ask me to ring back?'

☐ I asked Hamish, 'Did he ask me to ring back?'

☐ I asked Hamish, 'Did he ask me to ring back?'?

2 Which sentence has the correct punctuation?

SHADE ONE BOX

☐ Enzo asked? 'What did Kara mean by that comment.'

☐ Enzo asked, 'What did Kara mean by that comment?'

☐ Enzo asked, 'What did Kara mean? By that comment?

☐ Enzo asked. 'What did Kara mean by that? Comment.'

3 Which sentence has the correct punctuation?

SHADE ONE BOX

☐ Whenever, Molly, goes to the city she visits her sister.

☐ Whenever Molly, goes to the city she visits her sister.

☐ Whenever Molly goes to the city she visits her sister.

☐ Whenever Molly goes to the city, she visits her sister.

Shade one box to show where the missing apostrophe (') should go.

SHADE ONE BOX

4 I took my cameras to the party but could not get anyones attention long enough to frame the shots I wanted.

5 The brochures displayed images of an Olympians running shoes.

SHADE ONE BOX

6 In the wedding party, all the mens tuxedos sported exquisite roses in their lapels.

SHADE ONE BOX

Grammar

SHADE ONE BOX

1 Which of the following correctly completes the sentence?

The band was so extraordinary I ☐ listened to them until dawn arrived.

☐ could of ☐ couldve ☐ could've ☐ could'ave

9780170462860

2 Which of the following correctly completes the sentence?

SHADE ONE BOX

Tali knew that she [ ] brilliantly even before the final chord was struck.

☐ sings ☐ will sing ☐ has sung ☐ had sung

3 Which of the following correctly completes the sentence?

SHADE ONE BOX

Paddy, [ ] likely to be chosen for the team, is a very unassuming boy.

☐ whos ☐ whose ☐ who's ☐ whose'

Read the following text and answer the questions below.

The Loch Ness Monster

The Loch Ness Monster is one of the best-known species of cryptozoology. While there's been no physical evidence of its existence, lots of people claim to have seen the creature since it first came to attention in 1933, and it is affectionately referred to by the pet name 'Nessie'.

4 The text is written in the

SHADE ONE BOX

☐ past tense.
☐ present tense.
☐ future tense.

5 In this text the word 'Nessie' is in inverted commas because it is

SHADE ONE BOX

☐ a technical word.
☐ difficult to pronounce.
☐ a made-up word.
☐ a word from another language.

Reading – what's it all about?

When you think about it, reading is a strange thing – an array of symbols strung together from which we gain meaning and hear different voices 'speaking' in our heads!

But this strange thing is something we all do, every day, many times in an amazing variety of contexts: at the breakfast table, on the bus, in the car, at the train station, in the supermarket, in the classroom, using our music player walking down the street, at the cinema… Can you think of other places where you are engaged in reading?

What we read helps us live each day achieving what we want. In this sense reading is an essential life skill. But reading offers us so much more. Reading takes us places we haven't been; it helps us understand different people and the different ways they live their lives; and most of all it expands our sense of what is possible. What does reading offer you?

What happens when we read?

When we read our brain is working overtime:

- It is cracking a code.
- It is working out what the text means.
- It is working out the uses of the text.
- It is evaluating what the text does to the reader.

1 When we read we are unconsciously doing detective work – we are *breaking a code*.

   The code we are breaking is the code of the English language – letter / sound combinations, word / sentence structure, grammar and syntax, spelling and punctation. We use our knowledge of this code to establish a basic understanding of what the text is saying.

2 Working out what the text means involves us in comprehending the text we are reading. We do that on two levels – the *literal* and the *inferential*. In comprehending literally we are answering such questions as Who? When? Where? What? How?

   In comprehending inferentially the reader is asked to 'read between the lines', to make inferences about the messages being conveyed in the text. The meaning is implied but not precisely stated in the text. In working out the meaning of a text we bring our personal experience and background knowledge into play to assist us.

3 In working out how a text can be used we have to understand that the type of text and the purpose for which it has been written shapes both the content and the way that content is presented in the text.

4 Evaluating what the text does to the reader means that we see that texts are not neutral but represent particular points of view. They are put together in ways that attempt to influence readers in a particular direction.

In the Reading test you will draw on all these processes.

Stages of reading

To become a more effective reader you need to become more aware of what you are doing when you read.

Before reading

Survey the text so that you establish an overview of what you have in front of you.

1 Look at:
   - the title
   - the way the material is organised
   - headings and subheadings
   - graphs, diagrams, tables
   - quickly read the introduction and the first sentence in each paragraph.

2 Predict what the text is about.

3 Activate any knowledge you already possess that is relevant to this text.

4 Pose questions that you have about the topic.

As you read

1 Read actively – make notes, highlight parts of the text, make annotations, draw diagrams and maps to help you remember the main ideas and important details.

2 Connect new material with your prior knowledge.

3 Note key vocabulary.

4 Use context clues to work out words you don't know.

5 Monitor yourself – note areas that you don't understand.

6 Re-read sections you didn't understand on first reading.

7 Have your questions been answered?

After you read

1 Summarise the main ideas.

2 Represent the main ideas and their connections in a mind map / graphic organiser.

3 Integrate this new information with what you already know.

4 Work out how you can use this new information.

Simple to complex

The questions you will be asked to answer in the test will move from questions of basic comprehension to increasingly complex interpretive and inferential questions.

For example, on each text you will begin with straightforward 'where' and 'what' questions and phrases like:

'According to the text…', 'The words "as time passed" tell us that…' 'What is this text mainly about?'

The questions will then move to a more challenging level perhaps focusing on the use of inverted commas in the text, the use of figurative language or the purpose of the text.

Finally, more complex questions of interpretation and inference will appear like:

'Why did…'

and questions about the effect of using a particular style of writing (for example first person narrative), specific techniques employed for particular effects, selecting the main purpose of the text among a number of evident purposes.

Skills and understandings you need

1 **Skimming**
This involves looking quickly through a text to get the main idea. You use this technique to preview a passage before you read it in detail and to refresh your understanding of a passage after you've read it in detail.

2 **Scanning**
This involves moving your eye quickly over the page to find particular words or phrases that are relevant to the topic. It's useful to scan a text to see if irrelevant material is present.

3 **Locating topic sentences**
Identifying the topic sentence in each paragraph will help you with taking notes and selecting relevant information. Often, but not always, the topic sentence comes at the beginning of a paragraph.

4 **Detailed reading**
When you are reading in detail you are reading every word. Your aim is to make sure that you are gathering information from the text with 100% accuracy.

5 **Underlining / highlighting**
Underline or highlight what you consider are the most important parts of what you are reading. You might find it helpful to use different colours to highlight different aspects.

6 **Key words**
Make a note of the main headings as you read. Use one or two key words for each point.

7 **SQ3R – Survey, Question, Read, Recall, Review**
This technique can incorporate the specific skills above. It summarises a process that promotes effective and efficient reading.

Working with different text types

All texts are constructed. The different structures are referred to as text types. Knowing the difference helps us to recognise that the language conventions, layout or structure, and purpose are distinctive for the text type. The ability to visualise (in our head) the features of a text type, and how those features are arranged, is essential to understanding the constructed meaning, when we are reading.

Narrative

There are many types of narrative. They can be imaginary, factual or a combination of both. They may include mysteries, science fiction, romances, horror stories, adventure stories, fables, myths and legends, historical narratives, ballads, slice of life stories, personal experience. A narrative text includes such elements as a theme, plot, conflict(s), resolution, characters, and a setting.

Three key features of a narrative are:

- Characters – with clear personalities
- Dialogue – often but not always used
- Use of descriptive language – to create images in the reader's mind and enhance the story.

9780170462860

A narrative usually follows a structure like:

1 Introduction: in which the characters, setting and time of the story are established. Questions like Who? When? Where? are answered.

2 Conflict or problem: this usually involves the main character(s).

3 Resolution: there needs to be a resolution of the conflict or problem. It may be resolved happily or unhappily.

What examples of narratives can you think of?

Recount

Recounts retell or recall a past event or story. Recounts begin by telling the reader things like what happened, who was involved, where this event took place, when it happened and why it occurred. This is called the orientation. The sequence of events is then described in some sort of order (for example time). The thoughts and feelings of the participants in the event(s) are described to show how their actions have been shaped by the experience. Details are provided without unnecessary descriptions. The ending provides a brief summary. Recounts can be:

- Factual – for example, a news story
- Procedural – for example, explaining how you went about completing a specific task
- Personal – an account of your last holiday.

Exposition

An exposition is used to develop an argument, which presents a point of view in a logical order. It argues a case for or against a particular position. Examples of exposition texts can include debates, editorials, arguments and advertisements.

The three parts of an exposition are:

- an introductory statement – that presents the writer's point of view and previews the arguments to be presented.
- a number of arguments – these aim to persuade the reader. A new paragraph is used for each new argument.
- A conclusion sums up arguments and reinforces the writer's point of view.

Information

An informative text is non-fiction text, which presents factual information to report or describe something. A newspaper article might give you information about a health issue like giving up smoking; a website might give you information about a movie; a notice from school might be advising you about what you need to take on an excursion.

Sentences are simple or compound to keep the meaning clear. Repetition is avoided. Information texts are usually written in third person and present tense. Information texts are everywhere and provide us with factual information. The opening paragraph usually provides a general overview followed by paragraphs that provide detailed descriptions and a summary in conclusion.

Key terms: context, dialogue, exposition, inference, information, narrative, point of view, punctuation, purpose, recount, scanning, sequencing, skimming, structure, syntax, topic sentence. See the Glossary on page 107 for definitions of these terms.

TEST 2: Reading

Instructions

- A correct answer scores 1 mark, and an incorrect answer scores 0.
- Marks are not deducted for incorrect answers.
- No marks will be given if more than the required number of boxes are shaded (most questions require one answer).
- Choose the alternative which most correctly answers the question and shade in the box next to it.

Section A: Narrative

Read the following narrative and then answer the questions that follow.

An African Folktale

Every evening, the *tajiri*, or the rich man, sat down to a hearty meal prepared for him in his own kitchen. The food that was left over would have been enough to feed a whole family, but the *tajiri* was extremely stingy. The leftovers from his table went to fatten his pigs so that he would have the benefit of them later.

The *maskini*, or poor man, lived on simple fare. He owned a goat that gave him milk and cheese, but his evening meal was usually nothing more than a bowl of porridge. However, he had found a way to make it more enjoyable. He would eat his meal while hidden outside the *tajiri*'s kitchen, where wonderful smells came wafting through the open window. They made the *maskini*'s mouth water, and the porridge seemed like a feast.

One evening the *tajiri* decided to take a walk in his garden in order to work up an appetite for dinner. He saw the *maskini* sitting outside the kitchen window. As the *tajiri* watched, he saw the *maskini* inhale deeply, and a blissful look come over his face. How dare he help himself to my smells, thought the *tajiri*, and he ordered his servants to seize the *maskini* and escort him to the village jail.

A few days later the *maskini* was summoned before the court that met weekly in the village center, where the case would be decided on its merits. The *tajiri* explained that the smells from the kitchen belonged to him, and the *maskini* was depriving him of them. As payment, he demanded the *maskini*'s goat, which was the only thing he owned. When asked to respond, the *maskini* looking very forlorn, could only stare at the ground and shuffle his feet, afraid to speak. The village elders, who had been hearing the case, now withdrew to the shade of the nearby baobab tree. After a brief discussion, the village chief came forward and addressed the crowd.

'The *maskini* did help himself to the smells from the *tajiri*'s kitchen,' she said. 'However, he did not receive any food from him. We have concluded, therefore, that the *tajiri* should not be given the goat. However, in fairness to him we believe he should have the right to smell the *maskini*'s goat whenever he wants.'

The *tajiri* was furious and left without saying a word. But the people of the village approved the court's decision. They felt that justice had been done.

Shade the correct box to answer the following questions:

1 The *tajiri* sent the leftovers from his table to his pigs because

SHADE ONE BOX

- ☐ the pigs were his much loved pets.
- ☐ he didn't think his servants were hungry.
- ☐ he wanted to fatten his pigs for the future.
- ☐ he couldn't be seen to be favouring one poor family over another.

2 The *maskini* ate porridge in the evening because

SHADE ONE BOX

- ☐ it was good for his digestion.
- ☐ it took all day for the porridge to be prepared.
- ☐ that was all that was left at the end of the day.
- ☐ it was his tribe's customs to eat porridge at night.

3 The porridge seemed like a feast tells us that the *maskini*

SHADE ONE BOX

- ☐ had very poor tastebuds.
- ☐ wanted to trick the *tajiri.*
- ☐ knows the meal is a real treat.
- ☐ was able to convince himself it was good.

4 The *tajiri* sent the *maskini* to the village jail because

SHADE ONE BOX

- ☐ he wanted to brag to the villagers.
- ☐ the *maskini* had stolen something he owned.
- ☐ the *maskini* was trespassing on his property.
- ☐ the *tajiri* thought he owned the *maskini*'s goat.

5 The *tajiri* was furious because

SHADE ONE BOX

- ☐ the court had tricked him.
- ☐ the court didn't agree with him.
- ☐ the court had made an unlawful decision.
- ☐ he felt the court had misunderstood what he was asking for.

6 The people of the village felt justice had been done because

SHADE ONE BOX

- ☐ the court had made a decision.
- ☐ the *tajiri* didn't argue with the court.
- ☐ the *tajiri*'s greed had been highlighted.
- ☐ the court found the *maskini* guilty of the *tajiri*'s charge.

9780170462860

Section B: Recount

Read the following recount and then answer the questions that follow.

Paddock Surfing

Astrid Hildebrand, *Heywire* blog post | November 2008

In a small country town there is not a lot of standard recreational activity. In fact, very little is available in the way of movie theatres, shopping malls, swimming pools or any of those venues where average urban teenagers tend to collect to hang out with each other. This does not mean, however, that we country kids do nothing in our spare time. Rather, I like to believe it tends to challenge us, to bring out the more experimental and creative side in we young folk from the bush. My own adolescence was coloured by various forms of what must be designated 'extreme sports'. Leaping the fire, burning the witch, cowpat handicaps (and yes – that was a particularly grubby pursuit). And – my very personal favourite – paddock surfing. The latter was a truly inspired activity. Let me give you a glimpse. Take a ute – a rope and an old door. Add a freshly irrigated paddock (these are getting scarce nowadays mind you) and a bunch of uncivilised, energy supercharged adolescents and hey presto – you have all the essential ingredients for a 'good old time'. Picture this. The rope ties the door to the ute's towbar – and as many kids as possible cram onto the door. One older and slightly more responsible young turk mans the gearshift – and off you go! Shrieking, sodden, supernovaswift-slicing through the watery paddocks. The driver spins the wheel to accelerate the excitement, ducking and weaving from side to side. Kids squeal at the hint of danger, grab in wild attempts to hang on to that crazy super surfboard. Let's put this in perspective. Paddocksurfing is a bizarre, homegrown blend of more widely recognised 'sexy' activities like wake and snowboarding. But hey – we dreamed up this grubbier pastime all on our own one quiet Spring evening when there just didn't seem much to do. Yes – our friends from the farm down the road, my sisters and I dredged down deep in our imaginations and voila! Created our very own species of weird entertainment. Looking back now, as far as I'm concerned we really did come up trumps. Things are different these days. Now the paddocks are drought-dry and the idea of using waterladen paddocks for this type of entertainment seem lightyears away. But I'll never forget that country kids like us knew how to make something out of nothing. And I'll never forget the thrill of those wild, wild rides.

Shade the correct box to answer the following questions:

1 The writer thinks country kids

SHADE ONE BOX

- ☐ are foolish and take risks.
- ☐ are much smarter than city kids.
- ☐ need to be creative and imaginative.
- ☐ aren't as interested in entertainment.

2 According to the text, one of the challenges country kids face is

SHADE ONE BOX

- ☐ having lots of chores to do if they live on a farm.
- ☐ a lack of reliable transport available to get to venues.
- ☐ not seeing latest release films when they first come on.
- ☐ finding alternative forms of entertainment to the traditional ones.

3 'Looking back now, as far as I'm concerned we really did come up trumps.'

This suggests the writer thinks

SHADE ONE BOX

☐ they took a gamble and lost.

☐ that against the odds they achieved a good outcome.

☐ their most popular pastime was card games.

☐ after paddock surfing they had many cuts and bruises.

4 For the writer, paddock surfing represents

SHADE ONE BOX

☐ a good way to pass the time.

☐ the foolishness of childhood.

☐ the ingenuity of country kids.

☐ the failure of country kids to assess risk adequately.

5 My own adolescence was coloured by various forms of what must be designated 'extreme sports'.

SHADE ONE BOX

Why are the words 'extreme sports' in inverted commas?

This shows that

☐ they are spoken words.

☐ it is informal speech or slang.

☐ they are the most important words in the sentence.

☐ it is not the literal use of the words.

Section C: Expository

Read the following expository text and then answer the questions that follow.

Baz Luhrmann's *Australia* is Good, but not a Masterpiece

David Stratton, *The Australian* | November 18, 2008

Baz Luhrmann's eagerly awaited Australia is certainly the epic that we all expected.

It's very ambitious, it has enormous sweep and scope as it tells a story that takes place in the Northern Territory between 1939 and 1941...

...The second half of the story, after the inevitable love affair, involves the Japanese attack on Darwin and all its ramifications. Like his earlier films *Strictly Ballroom*, *Romeo+Juliet* and *Moulin Rouge*, *Australia* shows Baz Luhrmann as a very theatrical director. He has a great eye for compositions and the film is beautifully shot by Mandy Walker, but there's theatricality about the film which is a bit off-putting at the beginning. The early scenes, even the first 20 minutes or so of the film, are handled in a slightly artificial, arch manner which doesn't sit well with the outback locations and the natural settings of the story. It's all very well to be artificial when you're dealing with a theatrical concept like *Moulin Rouge* or even *Strictly Ballroom*, but it doesn't really work so well when you're

9780170462860

doing the same sort of thing here, so there's something that's just a little bit off key about these scenes. Then once the cattle drive gets under way either you get used to it or that aspect of it is played down because the remainder of the film is much stronger in a rather conventional way. I have to say, there's a lot of clichés in the script, a lot of familiar elements from other films of the past – *The Wizard of Oz* and the song 'Over the Rainbow' are heavily referenced – and it's as though the film is aimed at not so much an Australian audience but an international audience, and especially an American audience. I think probably it has the potential to be quite successful in America because it is, I think for Australians, a rather simplistic view of this whole period. It's the sort of film where if you make a point about half-caste Aboriginals in the first 10 minutes you have to restate exactly the same point another couple of hours further on. The film is not without flaws, it's not the masterpiece that we were hoping for, but I think you could say that it's a very good film in many ways. While it will be very popular with many people I think there's a slight air of disappointment after it all. But I will say that the acting is of a very high level, especially given that some of the actors have been encouraged to perform in this rather stylised, theatrical way...

...Despite its flaws – and it certainly has flaws – I think *Australia* is an impressive and important film, and if I were to give it a star rating I would give it three and a half out of five.

Shade the correct box to answer the following questions:

1 David Stratton thinks the film *Australia* is

SHADE ONE BOX

- ☐ a masterpiece.
- ☐ a failure and disaster.
- ☐ a very good film despite its flaws.
- ☐ a film you shouldn't bother going to see.

2 Stratton suggests the film will appeal to Americans because

SHADE ONE BOX

- ☐ it has many cowboy elements in it.
- ☐ it presents a simplistic view of the period.
- ☐ it uses a favourite American song, 'Over the Rainbow'.
- ☐ the actors speak with accents that can be understood by Americans.

3 According to Stratton, one of the film's greatest strength is

SHADE ONE BOX

- ☐ the cattle drive.
- ☐ its first 20 minutes.
- ☐ the quality of the acting.
- ☐ that it repeats important points.

4 Stratton is critical of the theatricality of the film because

SHADE ONE BOX

- ☐ the approach doesn't match the setting.
- ☐ the approach isn't kept up throughout the film.
- ☐ it makes the audience laugh at inappropriate times.
- ☐ the style isn't consistent with conventional approaches.

5 Stratton says in speaking of the film: 'It's very ambitious, it has enormous sweep and scope…'
The phrase 'sweep and scope' refers to

SHADE ONE BOX

- ☐ the number of actors in the film.
- ☐ the length and quality of the film.
- ☐ the setting and concerns of the film.
- ☐ the age groups the film will appeal to.

Section D: Informative

Read the following informative text and then answer the questions that follow.

Swimmers Happier in Another Skin

Leigh Dayton, *The Australian* | March 26, 2008

The body parts that make men men and women women are a real drag for elite swimmers, slowing their performances by fractions of a second…

…"The fat layer of the leg moves like a wave down their leg. One of the things the suit is intended to do is cut that movement down to avoid the drag," Mason said of the new Speedo bodysuit that's causing ripples in swimming circles.

Very simply, drag occurs when the water grabs swimmers, slowing them in their progress.

It's caused by the surface of the swimmer – their skin or the material of their swimsuit – and their shape.

That's why the LZR Racer suit was designed…Speedo claims its paper-thin designer fabric cuts surface drag. So too does the orientation of seams…because if they cut across the flow of water they increase turbulence and, therefore, drag. But as Tim Langrish, a Sydney University engineer with expertise in fluid dynamics, noted, no matter how good a suit looks technically, swimmers must be able to wear it and swim in it.

"It's a trade-off between physics and biology," Langrish said.

According to Mason, that was precisely the problem with prototypes of the new supersuit…

…"We discovered problems," (Mason) said. "If (the suit) restricted movement around the shoulders, reducing drag, it also reduced the ability to increase propulsion.

"It's also no good being so tight, it takes two hours to get into … these are the trade-offs. That's why it takes so long to develop (a suit)."

But the results, claim Speedo, offer a winning edge over its previous high-performance suits, reducing drag…

…Australia's head swimming coach Alan Thompson believes the spate of world records, which are being attributed to the new technology, has just begun as other leading countries prepare to hold their Olympic trials.

9780170462860

Thompson does not credit the fast times to the new swimsuits despite 13 world records in six weeks since they were launched.

"We are having great performances here [at the national Olympic trials] and, in Europe, we saw a lot of world records broken over the last six days," Thompson said.

"I think it's a great performance of swimming and I think we have more to look forward to ... this is the Olympic year and that's what we expect."

Shade the correct box to answer the following questions:

1 According to the text, the times of elite swimmers are most affected by

SHADE ONE BOX

- ☐ the quality of pool water.
- ☐ the swimmers' own bodies.
- ☐ the materials used on pool surfaces.
- ☐ the mental approach of the swimmer.

2 According to the text, the swimsuit is designed to

SHADE ONE BOX

- ☐ look stylish.
- ☐ make swimmers look thin.
- ☐ cut surface drag in the water.
- ☐ increase swimmer comfort in the water.

3 Alan Thompson attributes the recent spate of world records to

SHADE ONE BOX

- ☐ the new swimsuits.
- ☐ 'faster' water in pools.
- ☐ better coaching methods.
- ☐ elite swimmers being well prepared.

4 It takes a long time to develop a suit because

SHADE ONE BOX

- ☐ a balance between physics and biology has to be struck.
- ☐ the material is very difficult to manufacture.
- ☐ funding for research and development in sport is scarce.
- ☐ elite swimmers are very critical when they trial the suits.

5 The title of the text is *Swimmers Happier in Another Skin*.
This suggests that

SHADE ONE BOX

- ☐ elite swimmers are impossible to please.
- ☐ elite swimmers are keen to use the new swimsuit.
- ☐ elite swimmers are unhappy with the new swimsuit.
- ☐ elite swimmers prefer swimming in a traditional swimsuit.

Key Skills: Writing

As part of the test you will be asked to write a piece of continuous prose. You are being assessed on how well you are able to fulfil the criteria used to mark your prose.

You will only be asked to write **one** type of text. You will have 40 minutes in which to write. Five minutes for planning, 30 minutes for writing and five minutes for editing is the recommended allocation of time.

The marker is assessing your ability to write a particular text type, either a **narrative, exposition, recount or informative** piece based on a theme supported by visual stimulus.

The Test

You will be instructed to write a particular text type (narrative OR exposition OR recount OR informative text).

You will be given suggestions for the ideas for writing including a general guide for structure and hints for the writing process.

The writing instructions will appear on a stimulus page. On the page will be images to inspire your response.

You must write about the **idea** related to the stimulus. You do not need to write about everything on the stimulus. You do not need to refer specifically to an image in your text.

Text Types

A narrative

Genres: short story, biography, autobiography, diary, letters

Structure: The orientation or introduction should establish character and setting followed by a complication that might arise for your character given either your character's nature, the setting or an event. Your story may reach a climax and the complication may be resolved.

Avoid unsatisfying resolutions such as waking from a dream.

Language conventions: To engage your reader use language that will build character and set the scene. Consider using **figurative language** such as similes, metaphors and personification. Using direct speech, a variety of attributions, vocabulary, pronoun references and appropriate register for speech can help with characterisation. The correct tense as well as action verbs and noun groups can help to build a story. First or third person narratives are the most common.

Activity for narrative

To enhance a narrative, a writer might appeal to the audience's senses when describing something. The writer influences the audience by using linguistic strategies such as similes, metaphors, personification and alliteration.

One way to practice this skill is to write a description of something. Choose a colour. Now describe that colour to someone who has not seen it before, making reference to the five senses. In the space provided below, practise using figurative language and devices of sound in your description of a colour. For example the colour light pink feels like the soft, springy touch of freshly wound fairy floss.

Colour: ______________________________

Description: ______________________________

____

____

____

Example narrative writing question:

Today you are going to write a narrative or story. The idea for your story might be … (look at stimulus).

You could write a story about …

It could be a story that …

Your story could consider …

Think about

- the characters and where they are
- the complication or the problem
- how this complication or problem will be solved
- how the story will end.

Remember to

- write a plan for the story
- write in sentences
- look at your choice of words, spelling, punctuation and use of paragraphs
- give your story a title
- check and edit your work when you have finished writing.

An exposition

Genres: argument, feature article, debate, persuasive speech, letter to the editor, public address, analysis, review – book or film, website, play, movie flyer

Structure: The first paragraph is the **introduction**, which gives a context for the content of the particular exposition and states the writer's argument or statement of point of view. An exposition explores that point of view using **clear points**. Each new substantial point will become the topic of a new paragraph. The writer will use **evidence** to support each point being made. The end or **conclusion**, also its own paragraph, will summarise the points and restate the central argument.

Language conventions: Expositions are usually written in first person or third person. Writers use language of persuasion or argument. The text has a sense of immediacy and it is for this reason that the present tense of verbs is often used. Where appropriate, strategies such as rhetorical question, accumulation, alliteration, repetition and some figurative language can be used. A writer must select evidence to validate or support the points presented.

Activity for exposition

One way to practice structuring an exposition is to write the topics for an **argument**. Make a statement and then find three reasons why your statement is true. These reasons would become the topic sentences in an exposition. A topic sentence is one sentence and does not include examples or evidence.

Try finding three topics for the following statement.

Statement: The school uniforms should be changed to the colour ________________.

Topic One: ________________________________

Topic Two: ________________________________

Topic Three: ________________________________

Conclusion: Therefore the school uniform should be changed to ________________________________

Example exposition writing question:

Today you are going to write an expository text. The idea for your exposition is … [look at stimulus]

Your exposition might be an argumentative essay about … [suggestion for writing will appear here]

It could be the text of a persuasive speech or public address about …[suggestion for writing will appear here]

You could write a review about …[suggestion for writing will appear here]

… encouraging an audience to feel a particular way about it.

Think about

- the central argument you are making
- the logical, relevant points that support your argument
- the conclusion you will draw at the end of your argument.

Remember to

- write a plan for your text
- write in sentences
- look at your choice of words, spelling, punctuation and use of paragraphs
- check and edit your work when you have finished writing.

A recount

Genres: an historical text, biography, autobiography, an interview with an eyewitness, journal or log, blog.

Structure: In the **introduction**, the writer reveals in chronological order who, what, where and when. The body of the recount includes the **retelling of events** expanding on the detail of the introduction. Some elements of **reflection** can also be used to evaluate events and offer insight into the writer's attitudes, values and beliefs. A **conclusion** is a brief summary of what has been recounted.

Language conventions: When selecting cohesive ties for a recount the writer uses those associated with time such as then, after, another, following, next. Beware of overusing the word 'then' in a sequence of events. This form of writing relies less on figurative language and while it may contain some references to the present tense, it is predominantly written in the past tense and in first person.

Activity for recount:

You have been asked to write a **diary** entry noting in chronological order the four times you have seen or noticed the colour you nominated in the activity for the narrative and the exposition. Note how seeing that colour made you feel.

The first time I saw the colour ________________.

____

____

____

____

9780170462860

Example recount writing question:

Today you are going to write a recount. The idea for your recount is ... [look at stimulus]

Your recount might be an eyewitness account of a person, place, thing, action or idea in the stimulus.

It could be a journal kept by someone observing or keeping a record about a person, place, thing, action or idea in the stimulus.

A record of what you saw, felt, heard, touched, tasted and remembered.

Think about

- the central idea or point of your recount
- the sequencing of events in the recount
- the conclusion or final point of the recount.

Remember to

- write a plan for the recount
- write in sentences
- look at your choice of words, spelling, punctuation and use of paragraphs
- check and edit your work when you have finished writing.

An informative text

Genres: newspaper article, scientific report, medical examination, instructions, manual

Structure: Information texts are to impart facts to its readers. The **introduction** or first paragraph is a general overview of the purpose of the content of the information. Information is grouped in a logical way into **separate paragraphs** and usually ordered from most to least interesting and important. A short summary of the information or final point may be in the final paragraph or **conclusion**.

Language conventions: Language choices are subject specific, perhaps including technical language. The writer may choose to use sub headings or dot points where relevant. Sentences are simple and compound and usually written in third person in present tense.

Activity for informative text

Think about the instructions for making something; identify at least three different aspects to the instructions. For example, you might write instructions for a paint-making manufacturer telling them how to make the colour you have been using in the earlier activities using raw materials from nature. The body might follow this plan. Paragraph **1** where the colour in nature can be found; paragraph **2** how the colour can be extracted from the natural product; and paragraph **3** how it can be made into a paste suitable to add to a paint.

Example informative text question:

Today you are going to write an informative text. The idea for your informative text is ... [look at stimulus]

You might write a news article report on ...

You could write a report for a journal on what you have found out about ...

You might write a 'how to' guide for ...

Think about

- the central idea or focal point of the informative text
- the logical sequence to report the information
- the conclusion.

Remember to

- plan the sequence and content of the information
- write in sentences
- look at your choice of words, spelling, punctuation and use of paragraphs
- check and edit your work when you have finished writing.

The Criteria for Assessment

When planning and writing your work, consider the following:

Audience – These are the people to whom your work should appeal. The marker will expect **certain qualities** in your writing depending on the style/genre and content. How well the audience **engages** with, and is **influenced** by your work will be affected by the choices you as the writer make.

Character and setting – As not all stories rely on both characters and setting, the writer will only be assessed on that which is critical to the narrative. How well you construct and create these elements to affect your audience is assessed in this criterion.

Cohesion – A cohesive piece of writing contains ideas that **interconnect**, develop and link in a way that is appropriate to the genre and purpose.

Ideas – In accordance with the genre, you will be assessed on how well you have **selected**, **developed** and **explored** a range of appropriate ideas to fulfil your purpose. Consider the complexity and sophistication of the ideas.

Paragraphing – How well and accurately you use paragraphs to help your reader understand your text and development of ideas is assessed by this criterion.

Punctuation – Use accurate punctuation to aid the reader's understanding of the text.

To enhance the writing and demonstrate your ability to use a range of punctuation, employ a variety of sentence constructions that require different forms of punctuation (such as direct speech, commas for clauses, phrases, semi-colons and dashes) punctuated **accurately** and used in the right **context**.

Sentence structure – How well and **grammatically accurately** you have constructed a **range** of sentence types to suit your purpose is assessed by this criterion.

Spelling – Accurate spelling of a range of simple, common, difficult and challenging words will be assessed.

Text structure – When writing you need to organise the text in accordance with the genre and the needs of your audience.

Vocabulary – Consider the **range**, **complexity** and **appropriateness** of words chosen in order to most effectively achieve your purpose.

Key terms: alliteration, climax, cohesion, context, exposition, first person, inference, informative, language conventions, narrative, point of view, metaphor, personification, punctuation, purpose, rhetorical question, recount, simile, structure, third person, tense, topic sentence. See the Glossary on page 107 for definitions of these terms.

9780170462860

Example Test: Annotated responses

Instructions

- A sample writing stimulus has been provided on this page and the next.
- Read the following annotated responses to see examples of each of the Informative, Narrative, Recount and Expository writing genres.

Look at the following stimulus. (Note that in the actual test, only **one** text type option will appear.)

You are going to write a narrative or story.

The idea for your narrative is 'Australia'.

You could write a story about a character facing a uniquely Australian problem.

It could be a story where an Australian setting has an influence on a character.

Your story could consider the nature or impact of an Australian way of life.

Think about
- the characters and where they are
- the complication or the problem
- how this complication or problem will be solved
- how the story will end
- write a plan for the story.

Remember to
- write in sentences
- look at your choice of words, spelling, punctuation and use of paragraphs
- give your story a title
- check and edit your work when you have finished writing.

You are going to write an expository text.

The idea for your exposition is 'Australia'.

Your exposition might be an argumentative essay about a particular view about Australian people, place or life.

It could be the text of a persuasive speech or public address about an aspect of Australia.

You could write a review of a popular tourist destination that encourages tourists to visit.

Think about
- the central argument you are making
- the logical, relevant points that support your argument
- the conclusion you will draw at the end of your argument.

Remember to
- write a plan for the text
- write in sentences
- look at your choice of words, spelling, punctuation and use of paragraphs
- check and edit your work when you have finished writing.

You are going to write a recount.

The idea for your recount is 'Australia'.

Your recount might be an eyewitness account of a person, place, thing, action or idea in the stimulus.

It could be a journal kept by someone observing or keeping a record about a person, place, thing, action or idea in the stimulus.

Your recount could be a record of what you saw, felt, heard, touched, tasted and remembered about something on the stimulus.

Think about

- the central idea or point of your recount
- the sequencing of events in the recount
- the conclusion or final point of the recount.

Remember to

- write a plan for the recount
- write in sentences
- look at your choice of words, spelling, punctuation and use of paragraphs
- check and edit your work when you have finished writing.

You are going to write an informative text.

The idea for your story is 'Australia'.

You might write a news article reporting on a recent event (real or imaginary) that has happened in Australia.

Write a report for a journal on what you have learned about one aspect of Australia. (It could be a place, thing or idea like mateship.)

Write a 'how to' guide for something relevant to Australia and the stimulus.

Think about

- what is the central idea or focal point of the informative text
- the logical sequence of reporting the information
- the conclusion.

Remember to

- Write a plan for the sequence of information
- write in sentences
- look at your choice of words, spelling, punctuation and use of paragraphs
- check and edit your work when you have finished writing.

The writing process:
There are a range of images of Australia. After looking at the stimulus, **compile** a list like the one below of possible ways to view each image.

Image	Possible meanings
Sydney Opera House drawing	A souvenir, an image of the largest city, a destination, a cultural icon
Surf lifesaving flags and beach	Coastal living, the role of surf lifesavers, the dangers on our beaches, the beauty of the coastline
Uluru	A spiritual centre for some Aboriginal groups and tribes, the heart of Australia, a geological landform, an artist's inspiration, a tourist attraction
The outback and animal skull	Australia's outback, barren land, drought
Wild flower	Beautiful nature, medicinal quality, colour, fragility
Kangaroo	Symbol of the outback, traditional food of Australian Aboriginal people, image of Australian identity, biggest marsupial, pest
Meat pie	Australian cuisine or foods, foreign ownership of Australian foods, cultural icon, diet
Footwear	Australia fashion, heat

Now **look** at what you are asked to do.

1. What type of writing are you being asked to do (narrative or exposition or recount or information)?
2. What genre can you write in this style?
3. Which image best inspires you to write in that genre?
4. How might you incorporate the diverse ways of seeing Australia or one way of seeing Australia in your writing?

Look at the following texts. Each has responded to the same stimulus in each of the ways you might be asked to write.

Note the differences in genre and how this has influenced the choices made by the writer.

Narrative annotated example response

Use of title to guide audience understanding of theme and purpose.

Introduction of key characters, setting and context for narrative.

Use of past tense.

Sustained first person narration.

Short opening sentence to draw interest of audience.

First complication.

Use of direct speech to reveal character and tone of narrative.

The Treasure

Alliteration for emphasis and revelation of character.

Vocabulary selection relative to title and enhances cohesion and ideas.

I was **sent** away by **my dad**. I heard whispers and raised voices between Dad and Nanna catching bits of, "teenagers these days…. Ella just won't grow up," and "she's out of control – not keeping up at school – **she doesn't know how good she's got it**." Nanna's voice **seemed soothing** through the kitchen door as they agreed that I would move up to the big house and she would set me **right**.

Simple description to establish narrative setting. Selection of memorabilia is consistent.

Accurate spelling of difficult word.

As a kid I had loved visiting Nanna's and being allowed to roam and **explore** its rooms and secret verandah rooms crammed with the rusted tin toys of my dad's childhood, **rummaging** through his **boxes of cars, toy soldiers and dusty old school books** that Nanna had piled in old cardboard suitcases under unused beds.

Use of technical vocabulary associated with storage of old belongings. Cue for setting.

Recurring symbol for complexity of ideas.

Sneezing as I went from the **dust** and remains of **naphthalene** hunting for **treasure**, I always made little **discoveries** ; something small would be found that would give me a clue about the dad who found me so infuriating.

Vocabulary related to title and structure and sequencing and recurring symbol.

First use of title as foreshadowing to enhance ideas and cohesion.

The day I found his Year 7 copybook **buried** deep inside a **box** stuffed with **bits** and **bobs** of model cars and planes and **dried** up paint pots and sticks of craft glue and an assortment of metal bits from the main shed was a **discovery** of greater significance than I had first realised. Underneath all this **treasure** was the somewhat faded and worn book in which my father had written his lessons under the watchful eye of Nanna. She had been there to tune the radio, to guide her son (or so I had **thought**), as the lessons crackled over the airwaves from the School of the Air Base in **Rockhampton**.

Use of alliteration buried, box, bits, bobs for emphasis.

Repetition of vocabulary to reinforce story purpose for structure and sequencing as well as complexity of ideas.

"Why had the book found its way here?" I wondered aloud only to stop myself as the book fell open on my lap. It wasn't the caramel like smell of old paper, or the crude drawing of a horse in pencil on the page's top right hand corner that stopped my breath, it was the large handwriting, the awkward and misshapen letters that formed remnants of words that made me stare. **Who** could have written this scrawled and barely legible prose?

Use of recurring symbol for complexity of ideas and cohesion.

Use of paragraphs to introduce change in idea, thought or plot development.

Never one to let a **mystery** lie **unsolved**, I sprang to my feet scrambled over boxes and bounced down the long, polished hallway floor to the sitting room where Nanna sat, staring idly beyond the window at the **green** sugarcane crops dancing in the pre **storm**, afternoon breeze.

Second complication.

Use of recurring symbol for structure and complexity.

Use of recurring symbol that opposes the symbol of dust.

Use of symbol for climax and change.

Provides more detail about setting.

Use of language to reveal teenage character.

"What's this Nan? Could Dad not spell or something, cause he is always **like** getting up me about my school work," I stated almost a little too triumphantly.

Use of recurring symbol that opposes the symbol of dust.

Use of recurring symbol that opposes the symbol of dust.

She turned her gaze from the lush **green**, the **fertile** red dust that edged the crop and the grey sky that promised **rain**.

Use of ellipses for thought.

"Come," she said and beckoned me closer opening her wrinkled, **roughened** hands so that I might hold them like the innocent child I realize I must have seemed to her.

Use of vocabulary for characterisation.

"I know this book . . ." she mused and ran her freed hand over its dry, dusty cover, pushing the creases of brown paper to the edges of the book.

Use of different attributions for atmosphere and setting.

"It's like Dad couldn't read or write or anything," I **crooned** as I pulled my hand back to my lap.

"Sometimes, things can't be as we would want them," she replied, far too cryptically for my liking.

Use of recurring symbol that opposes the symbol of dust.

"Alright, you got me. Go on, I need to know."

Use of symbol of dust for complexity of ideas.

Reference to and use of stimulus.

Use of simile to provoke image.

Use of recurring symbol of dust for cohesion and ideas.

Alliteration for emphasis.

Gently, patiently she explained the life of a dad I never knew. The beautiful scene beyond the window, the **fertility** of the farm was not always that. "When Dad was little, the rain just didn't come. The crops did not come and the harshness of an **Australian drought dried** up the land much **like** age has dried the skin on my hands." She spoke with a wisdom that I had no seen or noticed before and it was then that I learnt of the horrors of starvation, the hardship for a boy on the edge of manhood who did not have time to learn, but had to work the unforgiving land, **parched** of any life. Working in a copybook, painting model cars were forgotten for the **sake of survival**. The desire to learn and play was **dried** up by time spent working to keep the family from ruin.

Use of recurring symbol of dust.

Use of metaphor.

Structuring reference for cohesion.

"The land and life may seem fertile now, but if you squander the opportunity to nourish yourself, to grow and reap the harvest **you** can't be all that you are. When you don't grow, parts of you die and are boxed up **and** not thought of for a very long **time, "she** said softly.

Correct punctuation of direct speech and use of new line.

Climax.

"You mean like me and school and what I have, don't you?" I responded in a higher, more irritated pitch than I had meant.

"Your life will follow cycles, much like the land here has its own cycles. Sometimes you will have the chance to be nourished and sometimes you will not," she said.

Resolution.

At that moment, the rain started to spatter against the window and Nanna's gaze turned back to the cane. I heard the **plish**, **splish** of the drops and for the first time I heard what Dad was trying to tell me about how I should make the most of now. Now **was** my time to grow.

Use of onomatopoeia.

Repetition for emphasis and cohesion.

I hadn't just opened his box of toys and stuff that day, I had opened the memory **of** a hardened life and the lesson I should take from it. That day I had found **treasure**.

Metaphor.

Structuring device – reference to title, metaphor.

Recount annotated example response

Journal of the Enlightened Tourist

Use of title to indicate purpose and style.

I'll never **forget** this blistering, hot January afternoon when my eyes beheld the **Rock** and I touched IT. Today I learned something that surpasses geology and tourism and uncovered the truth of the living heart of **Australia**.

First person recount.

Use of past tense.

Reference to stimulus.

Outline in introduction the sequence of recount.

It was the rich intense ochre, the blood-orange **hues** that captured my attention from the **very start**. My gaze was held like one in a trance around a campfire, inspiring my awe and forcing me to stand and stare, amazed at **Nature's** glorious creation. All those postcards from my friends who had visited the rock had prompted me to make this journey to see this geological icon, but I never imagined that those glossy cardboard reproductions of **"Uluru at Sunset"**, could possibly be real. Rather, I believed the postcards to be photo shopped images designed to entice me, the potential tourist, or at the very least inspire envy in all of us who wished we could be there.

Recount is in chronological order.

Note use of capital letter.

Correct use of quotation mark.

Vocabulary

And there I was today- eyes wide, mouth **agape** in front of that massive rock, reveling in the reality of those images and wondering if I too could get a shot that captured the colours just right. My unsophisticated camera with its 3 X zoom was no match for the awesome spectacle. In fact from up close I really couldn't fit the whole rock in. And this isn't the first time, because I remember the Pyramids all too well. I replaced my camera in my travel bag, took a long drink from my canteen and I am **noting** here that I will go on one of those motorbike tours and spot the rock from a **distance**.

Use of paragraphs to indicate change of thought, idea, or subject.

Vocabulary

Personal note to first person narrator – suitable for recount and journal.

Repetition of distance for cohesion.

Distance though would not allow me to do what I did **next**, which was to pick up a handful of red dust. Surely this was worn rock, rock dust that once formed the **skin** of the impressive wonder before me. As the dust wound its way **like a snake** through my fingers, I saw it move as though it had a life of its own. I did, I admit, toy with the idea of taking a little bit home that would serve as a remembrance, a souvenir of the rock. Surely, I did argue with myself, that taking a small handful wouldn't matter, it wouldn't be missed. I searched then for a little container amongst my belongings for something suitable in which to put the dust.

Connecting signal for chronology.

Use of personification.

Use of simile to provoke image.

It was **then** as I gazed up towards the rock that I saw it. A faint movement or beating could be seen in the heat waves which radiated from the rock's surface. It was at this moment I realized that that this is no ordinary landform. **IT** is alive.

Use of cue for recount.

Use of capital for emphasis.

9780170462860

Use of personification.

Variation of sentence constructions.

Embarrassed and ashamed that I thought… no that I dared to think to take something from this awesome **creature**, I then threw my open palm over, dusted my hands and roughly and quickly repacked my belongings. **Stumbling as I went,** head and eyes cast down, I backed away from the blood red earth and back to the path to join the group and that pedantic tour guide in the gift shop.

Short, relevant conclusion.

Personification/ reference to stimulus.

Overwhelmed I sit here writing this unable to imagine surpassing the moment I had today with **Uluru**.

Expository annotated example response

Environmental Impact of Domestic and Commercial Waste in Australia

Title to indicate purpose and relationship with stimulus.

Introductory paragraph.

Present tense.

Third person.

Thesis or controlling idea.

Outline of three points for argument.

Australia **is** a beautiful country resplendent with pristine beaches, spectacular landforms and is home to many endangered and unique species of flora and fauna. While the **nation** is home to these wonders, **the environment is at risk of destruction in the hands of a negligent population.** Evidence of the environmental impact of human beings is observable in the state of the **waterways, land and air quality**.

First topic sentence.

Uses technical vocabulary.

Use of evidence.

Use of difficult vocabulary.

Uses technical vocabulary and accurately spells difficult words.

Accurate use of commas in a list.

The waterways are in serious danger of environmental catastrophe as a result of industrial, waste and domestic rubbish. Factories built on the banks of **estuaries** are being held to account for dumping residue in waterways. Poisons and other toxins have seeped into the banks destroying species of native and endangered flora and causing outbreaks of disease within these plants. Similar to this has been the impact on the habitats of waterborne creatures interrupting delicate **ecosystems** and leading to the starvation and death of fish **species**. The flow on effect of diseased estuaries can be found in the oceans where the food sources of large fish species are being **depleted**. The impact of factory waste is compounded by the dumping of domestic rubbish. **Plastic bags, aluminum, tin and other rubbish** that is an eyesore, becomes an ideal breeding ground for dangerous bacteria that can cause disease and environmental harm and are readily consumed by native animals causing illness, disease and death.

Second topic sentence.

Linking device.

Reference to stimulus.

Not only is environmental devastation found in waterways. **Farming and bush land is equally at risk of becoming a poisonous wasteland as a result of hazardous landfill.** The serious ecological damage is as a result of waste that is not treated properly or correctly sealed. Unusable farm land, unable to sustain life is now becoming a problem as crops and pastureland in **Australia** is reducing at such a rate that food sources are depleting. Native animals are dieing as food is poisoned by toxic wastes seeping into the earth from toxins in waste dumped at landfill sites. Similar effects on crops are noted as the stunted growth of certain staples such as wheat are reducing harvests and food supplies. Diseases incubated by poisoned species are spreading to other areas of Australia via waterways, wind and birds and animals.

Third topic sentence.

Use of relevant vocabulary.

Linking device.

Linking phrase for cohesion.

The infected and fragile Australian landscape is being affected also by air pollution and the growing size of the hole in the ozone layer. The increasing use of aerosols such as insect sprays and deodorants are having a direct impact on the air. **In conjunction with this** domestic influence on the air, factory emissions of dangerous levels of sulphur and carbon monoxide are influencing flora and fauna. Air-borne diseases also affect food sources and other essentials to sustain life in Australia.

Conclusion.

Australians need to be aware of harmful pollution in our waterways and oceans, farming and bush land and air, and the impact that this is having on the country and the well being of its people, the flora and fauna. The harmful effect of household and industrial waste is diminishing necessary resources essential for the survival on an environment that can sustain **life**.

Reference to thesis and main topics.

Informative annotated example response

A Guide to Visiting Australian Beaches

Reference to stimulus.

Use of title and term guide to indicate style and purpose of informative text.

The beach is one of Australia's national wonders and is a popular tourist attraction. Many activities such as swimming, surfing, and ball games such as beach volleyball and cricket are enjoyed by locals and tourists. Though beautiful and inviting, beach goers are encouraged to take simple steps to ensure their day at the beach is memorable and safe.

Uses introduction to outline purpose of document.

Swimming alone, or on an unpatrolled beach **is** unsafe. The **number one rule** for a **fun time** at the beach is to **SWIM BETWEEN THE FLAGS**. Trained **lifeguards** mark the safest area in which to swim and place a yellow and red flag at each end of the patrolled section of the beach.

Present tense.

Use of accepted colloquial language.

Use of colloquial term for emphasis.

Use of capitals for emphasis.

By swimming between the flags **you** will be avoiding dangerous rips and any **hazardous** sandbanks. The water is also patrolled for other dangers such as stingers, sharks, crocodiles in the Northern Regions of Australia and unexpected hazards including motorized vessels and debris.

Use of relevant technical terms.

Use of paragraphs for each new point and short cohesive devices.

Accurate spelling of difficult word.

It is easy to recognise the lifeguards as they wear a distinctive uniform of a bright yellow shirt, red shorts and a red and yellow cap. Lifeguards patrol this flagged area of beach, watching swimmers and have necessary lifesaving equipment and administer **First Aid** should the need arise.

Use of second person in an information guide to address reader.

Use of technical language.

Logical development of ideas in order of importance.

In the flagged zone, you will be able to obtain from an information board or from the lifeguard current information such as tide times, wind directions and any current warnings that may have an impact on your day at the beach. You can also access basic **First Aid** from the lifesavers. You should always heed the advice provided by the lifesavers, follow their instructions and **use** your own judgment, **vigilance** and observations to help keep yourself safe.

Repetition of important detail.

Use of action verbs or commands.

Deliberate vocabulary choice.

Should you find yourself experiencing difficulty in the water and require the assistance of lifeguards, raise one arm and call for help. **A raised arm will attract attention and lifeguards will come to your aid.**

Use of short simple sentence for simplicity.

Use of numbers.

Use of colloquial expression through familiar slogan.

To lower your risk of future skin cancer, it is important to remain sunsafe. Try not to be out in the sun between **10am** and **2pm**. If this is impossible, follow the **'slip, slop, slap and wrap'** rule- slip on a shirt, slap on a hat, slop on some sunscreen and wrap on some sunglasses. The best way to stay protected is to wear protective clothing that covers your skin, use sunscreen with the highest UV protection number such as 30+ as a last measure of protection. Most sunscreens should be reapplied every 2 hours. Minimizing sun exposure and drinking water, can help you to avoid dehydration.

Imparting of facts.

9780170462860

By following the rules covered in this guide, being aware and prepared for a day at the beach, you can be sure to have a safe and enjoyable time at this most popular of Australian holiday destination.

Clear conclusion summarising main points.

Activity

For the texts you have just read, note the following:

Narrative

1. What was the point of the story?

____

____

2. Write down three examples of figurative language used in the story.

____

____

____

Recount

1. Outline the structure of the recount.

____

____

____

Exposition

1. Write down the thesis and the three topics in this expository essay.

____

____

____

____

Informative

1. What is the purpose of the information?

____

2. Write down, in order, the main points of the information.

____

____

____

____

Building

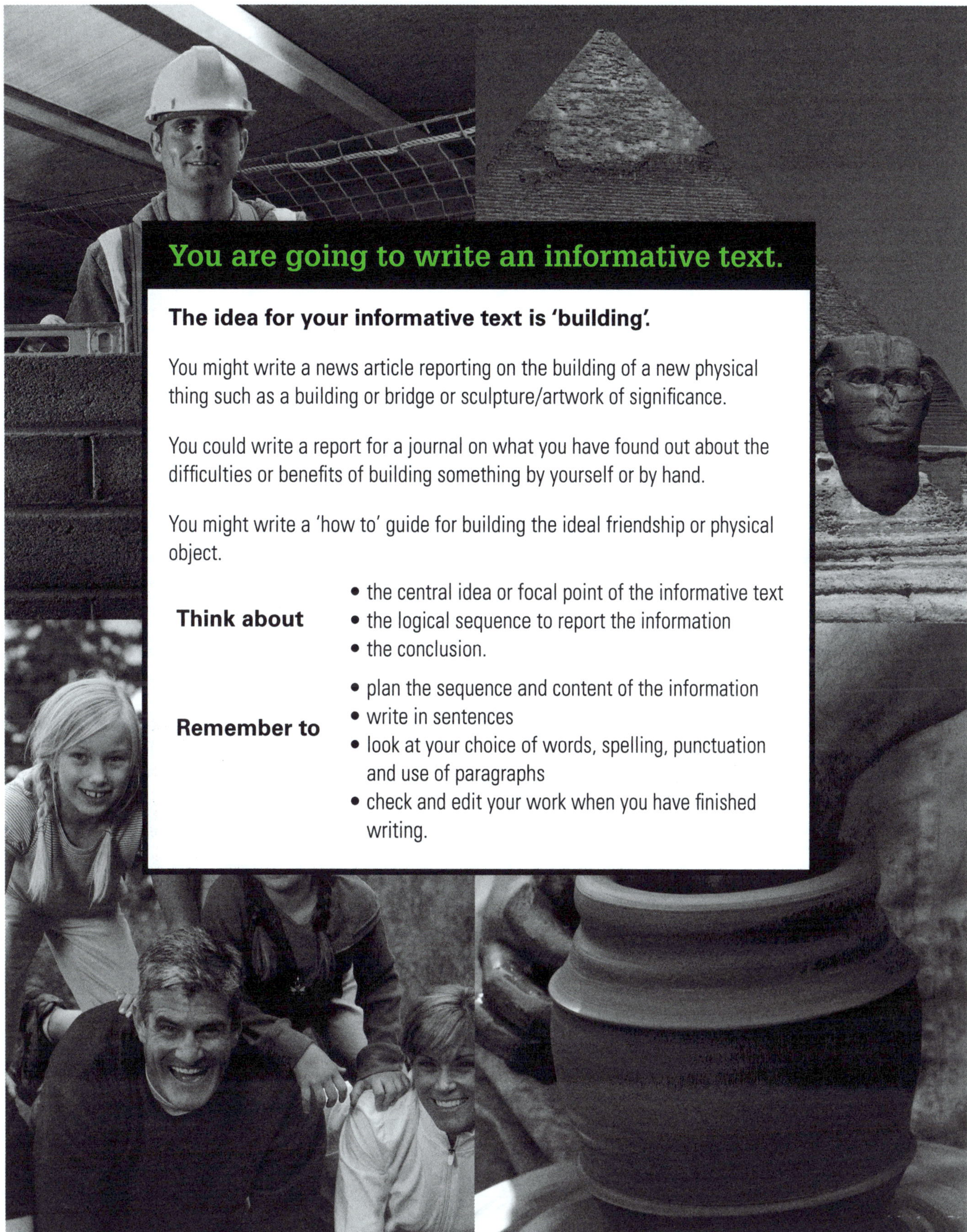

You are going to write an informative text.

The idea for your informative text is 'building'.

You might write a news article reporting on the building of a new physical thing such as a building or bridge or sculpture/artwork of significance.

You could write a report for a journal on what you have found out about the difficulties or benefits of building something by yourself or by hand.

You might write a 'how to' guide for building the ideal friendship or physical object.

Think about

- the central idea or focal point of the informative text
- the logical sequence to report the information
- the conclusion.

Remember to

- plan the sequence and content of the information
- write in sentences
- look at your choice of words, spelling, punctuation and use of paragraphs
- check and edit your work when you have finished writing.

Sample Writing Test – Informative

Look at the stimulus. Brainstorm your ideas and then use this box to write a clear plan. Allow no more than five minutes. This planning will not be marked.

Year 9 Literacy

Language Conventions Test 1

Writing time: 45 minutes

Use 2B pencil only

Instructions

- Write your **student name** in the space provided.
- You must be silent during the test.
- If you need to speak to the teacher, raise your hand. Do not speak to other students.
- Answer all questions using a 2B pencil.
- If you wish to change your answer, erase it very thoroughly and then write your new answer.

Student name:

The spelling mistakes in these texts have been circled. Write the correct spelling for each circled word in the box provided.

WRITE YOUR OWN ANSWER

1 The accomodation provided at the school camp is quite luxurius. In the past we have stayed in apalling conditions.

WRITE YOUR OWN ANSWER

2 We decided to visit the new portrate gallery. The presentation of each painting is spectacular. The lighting is impressive and emfasises the unique aspects of each piece. Gallery personel are available to provide additional information about the exibition.

WRITE YOUR OWN ANSWER

3 Regular daily exercise is vitle for our health now and in the future. Walk at a pace that increases your heart rate. Enjoy what your local enviroment has to offer.

Each sentence has one word that is incorrect. Write the correct spelling of the word in the box.

WRITE YOUR OWN ANSWER

4 The average tempratures have been higher than usual this summer.

5 A rather grand vesel is anchored in the bay.

6 Chocolate pudding is one of my top ten deserts.

7 Good rainfall at the right time results in a high crop yeeld.

8 It is a requirment of the club that you wear the correct uniform when playing.

9 Putting long hair into plats is no longer fashionable.

10 Next Saturday is open day at the navil base.

11 Once a committee agrees on a course of action they then have to impliment it.

Each sentence has one word that is incorrect.
Write the correct spelling of the word in the box.

WRITE YOUR OWN ANSWER

12 Alchohol should be taken in moderation.

13 It was a great coop to have the celebrity visit the school.

14 That teacher is very good at giving clear explainations.

15 There is secret ingreadient in that spaghetti sauce that makes it delicious.

16 Parlimentary procedures are quite complex.

17 The main character in that text has some severe psycological problems.

18 The climb to the sumit of Mount Everest is treacherous.

19 The tennis tornament will take the form of a round robin.

20 Which of the following correctly completes the sentence?

SHADE ONE BOX

Mark felt that he ☐ to the charity concert.

☐ should'ave gone ☐ should've gone ☐ should of gone ☐ shouldve gone

21 Which of the following correctly completes the sentence?

SHADE ONE BOX

Ricky has ☐ the drum kit he wants to get for his band at the local music shop.

☐ see ☐ saw ☐ seen ☐ will see

22 Which of the following correctly completes the sentence?

SHADE ONE BOX

Aisha, ☐ one of the best athletes on the team, will represent the state in the national championships.

☐ whose ☐ whose' ☐ whos ☐ who's

23 Which of the following has the correct punctuation?

SHADE ONE BOX

☐ Mary pleaded Jose. 'When am I going to see you?'
☐ Mary pleaded, 'Jose, when am I going to see you?'
☐ Mary pleaded, 'Jose when am I going to see you.'
☐ Mary pleaded, Jose when am I going to see you?

SHADE ONE BOX

24 Which of the following correctly completes the sentence?

Toan likes to ask teachers [ ] he calls 'curly' questions.

☐ when ☐ who ☐ what ☐ why

SHADE ONE BOX

25 Which of the following correctly completes the sentence?

Rowena said that she [ ] waited for him if he had sent her a text message.

☐ would of ☐ would'ree ☐ would've ☐ would'ave

SHADE ONE BOX

26 Shade one box to show where the missing apostrophe (') should go.

Only members of clubs are allowed to use the members entrance to the grounds.

SHADE ONE BOX

27 Which of the following correctly completes the sentence?

She examined the diamond ring [ ].

☐ really careful ☐ real careful ☐ really carefully ☐ real carefully

SHADE ONE BOX

28 Which of the following has the correct punctuation?

☐ Without the help, of our neighbours we wouldn't have had the house ready for inspection by Saturday.

☐ Without the help of our neighbours, we wouldn't have had the house ready for inspection by Saturday.

☐ Without the help of our neighbours, we wouldn't have had the house, ready for inspection by Saturday.

☐ Without the help of our neighbours we wouldn't have had the house ready for inspection, by Saturday.

SHADE ONE BOX

29 Which of the following correctly completes the sentence?

The drama group provided the audience with an [ ] performance.

☐ strenuous ☐ brilliant ☐ exceptional ☐ stunning

9780170462860

30 Which sentence has the correct punctuation?

SHADE ONE BOX

- ☐ 'I went skiing with the school' Nicky grinned. 'It was fantastic but really cold.'
- ☐ 'I went skiing with the school.' Nicky grinned, 'It was fantastic.' 'But really cold.'
- ☐ 'I went skiing with the school,' Nicky grinned. 'It was fantastic but really cold.'
- ☐ 'I went skiing with the school, Nicky grinned. It was fantastic but really cold.'

31 Which sentence has the correct punctuation?

SHADE ONE BOX

- ☐ So many students were late to school today; there must have been a traffic problem.
- ☐ So many students were late to school, today, there must have been a traffic problem.
- ☐ So many students were late to school today; there must have been a traffic problem?
- ☐ So many students were late to school today, there must have been a traffic problem?

38. Which of the following correctly completes the sentence?

SHADE ONE BOX

The ☐ offices are located in Mitchell Street.

☐ company's ☐ companies' ☐ companie's ☐ companies

32 Which sentence has the correct punctuation?

SHADE ONE BOX

- ☐ 'Oh really, said Mum, just get on with it!'
- ☐ 'Oh really,' said Mum. 'just get on with it!'
- ☐ 'Oh really,' said mum, 'just get on with it!'
- ☐ 'Oh really,' said Mum, 'just get on with it!'

33 Which sentence has the correct punctuation?

SHADE ONE BOX

- ☐ Mrs Rice said to try another method of solving the problem, so we used Peter's approach.
- ☐ Mrs Rice said, to try another method of solving the problem so we used Peter's approach.
- ☐ Mrs Rice said, 'to try another method of solving the problem, so we used Peter's approach.'
- ☐ Mrs Rice said, 'To try another method of solving the problem so we used Peter's approach.'

34 Which sentence has the correct punctuation?

SHADE ONE BOX

- [ ] He never enjoyed learning the violin, at school now he's the best in the orchestra.
- [ ] He never enjoyed learning the violin at school! now he's the best in the orchestra.
- [ ] He never enjoyed learning the violin at school; now he's the best in the orchestra.
- [ ] He never enjoyed learning the violin at school; now hes the best in the orchestra.

35 Which sentence has the correct punctuation?

SHADE ONE BOX

- [ ] She always enjoyed: sweets, chocolate, marshmallows and nougat.
- [ ] She always enjoyed sweets, chocolate, marshmallows and nougat.
- [ ] She always enjoyed sweet's, chocolate, marshmallows and nougat.
- [ ] She always enjoyed sweets chocolate marshmallows and nougat.

Read the following text and answer the questions below.

The Cavalier King Charles Spaniel

The ancestry of the Cavalier King Charles Spaniel can be traced back to the royal courts of England. King Charles II was devoted to his dogs – almost to the point of addiction. They travelled with him everywhere and the sign 'Beware of the Dog' originated in his court, meaning not that they were dangerous, but rather *don't tread on them*.

36 The text is written in the

SHADE ONE BOX

- [ ] past tense.
- [ ] present tense.
- [ ] future tense.

37 In this text the words 'Beware of the Dog' are in inverted commas because

SHADE ONE BOX

- [ ] they are a title.
- [ ] they are technical words.
- [ ] they are an actual quote.
- [ ] they are difficult to pronounce.

Read the following text and answer the questions below.

Olive Oil

Olive oil comes as plain olive oil, virgin olive oil, and extra-virgin olive oil. 'Virgin' refers to the quality of the olive oil; the more virgin it is, the better it is for you. Standard olive oil is darker in color, thicker, and burns less easily. Extra-virgin olive oil is clearer in color, has a distinct taste and is well suited for salad dressings.

38 In the first sentence the word 'olive' is used as

- ☐ a verb.
- ☐ a noun.
- ☐ an adjective.
- ☐ an adverb.

SHADE ONE BOX

39 This text has been written in the

- ☐ first person.
- ☐ second person.
- ☐ third person.

SHADE ONE BOX

40 In the third sentence the word 'easily' is used as

- ☐ a verb.
- ☐ a noun.
- ☐ an adjective.
- ☐ an adverb.

SHADE ONE BOX

Read the following text and answer the questions below.

Community Gardens

A community garden is a green space cultivated on common land by a group of people. Community gardens come in all shapes, sizes and situations. They can grow flowers, veggies, fruits or trees. They can be used as sustainable food resources, or just to look pretty. They can be on any kind of land in any city.

Australia's first community garden was built in Melbourne in 1977. Since then, the gardening bug has caught on, and now there are dozens of gardens in every state. Community gardens are supported by a variety of larger organisations, including the Australian Community Gardens network, Green Thumb, and in some states, even the department of housing.

41 In the second paragraph, 'the gardening bug' is an example of

SHADE ONE BOX

- ☐ a simile.
- ☐ a metaphor.
- ☐ alliteration.
- ☐ personification.

42 In the second sentence, 'shapes, sizes and situations' is an example of

SHADE ONE BOX

- ☐ exaggeration.
- ☐ a rhyme.
- ☐ a simile.
- ☐ alliteration.

43 In the opening sentence, the word 'community' is used as

SHADE ONE BOX

- ☐ a verb.
- ☐ a noun.
- ☐ an adverb.
- ☐ an adjective.

Year 9 Literacy

Reading Magazine 1

Animal Talk

Can animals talk?

Lots of animals can actually talk, but they communicate differently to the way that we do. Animals don't have a spoken language but instead they communicate with each other using sounds and gestures. That said, some animals (such as parrots and mynah birds) can make noises that sound like words, but they're actually just mimicking us and they don't really understand what they're saying.

How do animals talk and what do they say?

Well, birds chirp and sing, cats meow and purr, dogs bark, growl, whine and howl and dolphins click and whistle. This is all communication and probably means simple things like: 'I'm hungry', 'I'm annoyed' and 'I'm happy'.

Do they have conversations?

Possibly – some animal communication is very complex. For example, dolphins give each other instructions when they hunt fish together in groups and bees do a complicated little dance that tells other bees where they have found food. Some sea creatures including whales, dolphins and even the octopus and squid may have language much more complex than we realise. Cuttlefish, for example, can communicate with up to four other cuttlefish at once – by using different sides of their bodies to make patterns of light and colour. Whales have very complex songs that we don't understand, but as they have the biggest brains of any living creature, we figure they must use those big brains for something! As an example of just how big whale brains are, just remember that the next largest known creatures were the dinosaurs – and most large dinosaurs had brains the size of golf balls.

9780170462860

TEXT 2

Tung Ngo

I am an ordinary Australian young guy, and studying to be a teacher. I love my cricket and footy, pizzas from the local, and going to night clubs with my mates.

When I was 22 I ran for local council against the local National Front (a racist hate party) in Enfield in Adelaide, and won. I was sick of the hatred coming from some people and them saying that they represented the people, so I decided to stand up against it and find out who the people really supported. I spoke to a lot of people about this – and they all said if it was what I thought was right, then give it a go.

I faced racism and ignorance myself at school. I came to Australia as a refugee when I was 11 and was picked on heaps. Luckily, I had a teacher who was Greek and she understood what I was going through and really stood up for all of us who were different in some way. I stood up for myself too and after a while we got the bullies sorted. The hardest part for me was getting the English language. Once I had that it was much better – I could face up to the trouble-makers.

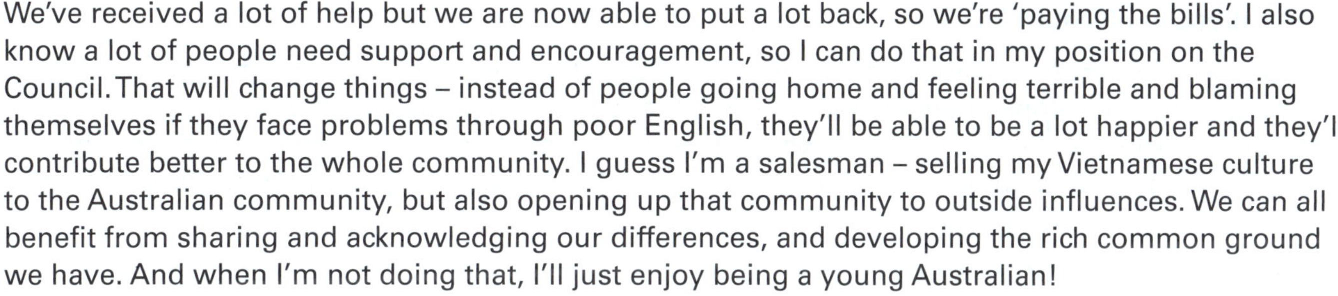
It's also important to put something back into the community. We've received a lot of help but we are now able to put a lot back, so we're 'paying the bills'. I also know a lot of people need support and encouragement, so I can do that in my position on the Council. That will change things – instead of people going home and feeling terrible and blaming themselves if they face problems through poor English, they'll be able to be a lot happier and they'll contribute better to the whole community. I guess I'm a salesman – selling my Vietnamese culture to the Australian community, but also opening up that community to outside influences. We can all benefit from sharing and acknowledging our differences, and developing the rich common ground we have. And when I'm not doing that, I'll just enjoy being a young Australian!

Fair Trade

What is fair trade?

The fair trade movement began in the late 1950s as an attempt to aid Chinese refugees in the US. Today, the International Fair Trade Association includes over one million producers and 3000 organisations in 50 countries.

Fair trade is a response to increasing globalisation. According to Oxfam and other fair trade advocates, large, developed nations like the US, UK and even Australia, pay their farmers to overproduce crops like coffee, corn and wheat. This overproduction drives crop prices down. The excess is then sold to underdeveloped or developing nations at absurdly low prices. This drives local farmers out of business, because they can't compete.

The fair trade movement aims to give these small local farmers a chance. Fair trade organisations work with local producers to sell goods on a global scale. Fair traders produce everything from earrings to chocolate to flour and wheat. So if you're in the market for an organic, ecologically and economically friendly cup of joe, an organisation can act as an agent between you and a coffee farmer in Honduras. Through fair trade, you can buy coffee from that farmer, and she or he will get most of the profits, instead of large corporations.

The fair trade movement also supports equal pay for women, eco-friendly modes of production and safe, healthy work environments.

In this way, the main goal of fair trading is to end world poverty by establishing millions of successful, independent, local producers in developing countries such as Ghana, India, Sri Lanka, Mexico and dozens more. Fair trade is now recognised by many as a way of combating global poverty.

Goha Gives His Son a Lesson

Goha had a son who was always worried about what people thought of him. The boy could never do anything because he thought other people would think he was foolish.

Goha wanted to teach his son that it was a waste of time to worry about the opinions of other people. He saddled his donkey and told his son he was going to a neighbouring village. Goha got on the donkey and asked his son to walk behind him. On the way they passed some people who pointed at Goha and said, "Look at that cruel man who rides his donkey and lets his son walk. He has no feelings."

When he heard this, Goha got off the donkey and asked his son to get on, while he himself walked. Again as they passed by, some people pointed at the boy and said:

"Just look at that boy who has no manners and rides that donkey while his old father has to walk."

Goha thought about this and decided they should both ride the donkey. So they both climbed onto the donkey's back and set off again. Again they passed by some people who pointed to them both riding on the donkey and said: "What a cruel man he is. He has no pity for his donkey and allows both him and his son to ride at the same time."

Again Goha thought about what the people had said and so he and his son got off the donkey. They both walked behind it. This time as they passed some people he heard them saying to themselves:

"What a couple of fools they are! Imagine walking when you have a donkey you could ride."

This time Goha was at a loss. Finally after a lot of thought he said to his son:

"Come on. Let's carry the donkey between us." So they lifted up the donkey and staggered along the road. Some people saw them and started laughing.

"Look at those two mad people, carrying their donkey instead of riding it!"

So they finally put the donkey down and Goha said to his son

"You must know my son, that whatever you do in life, you will never please everyone."

9780170462860

Preschool Teacher

Margaret Cook, 'Goodbye, Mr Toms...', *The Age* | December 1, 2008

For Kristin Cantwell, deciding to become a preschool teacher was instinctive – even in her teens.

'We had a family friend who worked in a preschool and talked about it. I liked what I heard,' she says. 'I'd also done babysitting and I liked young children.'

At 18, she enrolled at the Kindergarten Teachers College in Kew. Now 54, she is about to retire from her last job, Blue Hills Preschool in Bayswater. This is despite parents having 'begged, bribed and bullied' her to stay, according to the preschool's president, Tanya Young.

Since Mrs Cantwell graduated 33 years ago, she has worked in six centres, all in the City of Knox, with about 1700 children. 'Some are now nearly 40', she says, 'and many have children'.

During those years, Mrs Cantwell also raised four of her own children. The job is challenging but never boring – although she admits some parents ask her: 'How do you stay sane?'

'In one day, I'm an educator, psychologist, social worker, nurse, mentor, administrator, purchaser and cleaner,' she says. 'You need to have patience and tolerance, and be able to work through a child's inappropriate behaviour to understand the underlying reason why.'

Mrs Cantwell especially enjoys the honesty, innocence and enthusiasm of young children. 'They love you unconditionally and, apart from Mum and Dad, you're the most important person in their lives.'

Equally important is the respect that families give to preschool teachers. 'We're the first educational body they come to, and a big part of our job is working with them. Sometimes children are leaving their parents for the first time, and you get a lot of concerned Mums and Dads.'

Mrs Young says Mrs Cantwell is much loved by the children and has infinite patience.

'Preschool involves play-based learning', says Mrs Cantwell. 'For example, by playing with blocks, children learn about counting, size and shape. They also pick up pre-reading skills through songs, poems, listening to stories and making up their own.'

'However, it's not structured and each day, and each preschoool, is different. We work on each individual's learning and we plan the program around their interests and skills level: physical, emotional, cognitive and social.'

The aims are to promote a love of learning, encourage children to take responsibility for themselves and teach them skills they can use throughout their lives. During their year at preschool, they develop enormously, and this is another joy of the job.

TEXT 6

Think Twice Before You Slam That Can!

When we exercise we start to warm up, and as you get hotter your body starts to sweat.
If you're not careful sweating can drain your body of all the salts and water it needs to stay hydrated.

So after a big event you'll see lots of athletes drinking these. They're promoted as giving them lots more power than plain water. It's because they contain salts, carbohydrates and sugar to replace the important stuff your body needs to recover.

So if these drinks are so good for athletes they must be good for us, right?

Well, nutritionists say if you don't do much exercise and only play a bit of sport they're not the best thing for your body. You see if you don't burn up all those ingredients they'll just sit in your body – and turn into fat.

And if you don't enjoy going to the dentist you also might want to think twice. Studies have found drinking too many sports drinks can damage enamel on teeth and lead to decay.

Ouch!

But there is another group of drinks out there that looks just as exciting. Energy drinks are everywhere. Last year 3.5 billion cans of one particular brand of energy drink were sold in 140 countries.

So why are they so popular?

Like their name suggests, energy drinks give you – energy. But they use some different ingredients. Two are called caffeine and guarana. They're pretty funny names but they both come from plants and can be found in a lot of products.

Caffeine is in coffee, some teas and chocolate. Guarana is also in some snacks. They both stimulate your nerves and make you feel more alert. They can help people stay awake longer and are sometimes used by students when they're studying.

But there is a downside.

Doctors are worried that energy drinks could cause health problems. The concern has grown so much that energy drinks have been banned in France, Denmark and Norway.

Researchers have also just found that when people drank energy drinks their blood cells got sticky and clotted together. Once the blood sticks together it can block veins and arteries, which can lead to stroke or even death if someone has a weak heart.

There's more research that needs to be done but the advice is be careful about how much you drink. And next time you look into the fridge, take a second to think about what's really hiding behind the label.

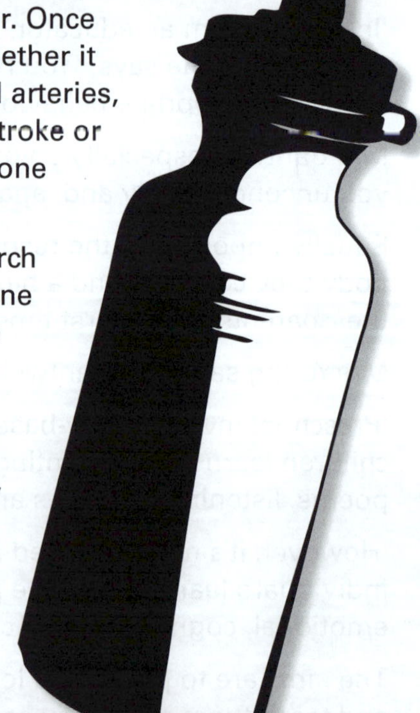

9780170462860

A Mistake

Lisa McNeice

I made a mistake when I was three or four:
I thought that Elvis Presley came to our house
and tuned my brother's ukulele.
Years later, during Love Me Tender, I turned to Mum
and said, remember when he...
And so I make my first quick click
of readjustment as a nine-year-old
sitting on our swirly loungeroom carpet.
Then just last night Dad told me of a kid
who had a room at the Eureka
and worked at the Post Office
he might have slept nights on the telephone exchange.
Not there long, but yeah, he did
look like Elvis come to think of it
and by crikey he could play the guitar.

Should We Ban Plastic Bags?

YES

Dear Sir/Madam,

I am writing in the hope that your readers will join the growing movement dedicated to seeing plastic bags banned from our lives. Plastic bags are a hazard to animal and human life and destructive of our environment.

Plastic bags are mistaken as food and consumed by a wide range of marine species, especially those that consume jellyfish or squid, which resemble plastic bags when floating in the water. In August 2000, an autopsy of a whale beached at Trinity Bay near Cairns revealed a tightly compacted ball of plastic debris in the animal's stomach. The contents included 33 different items made up mainly of plastic bags, as well as noodle packages. In total there was nearly six box metres of plastic in the whale's stomach.

Emissions associated with plastic bag manufacture and distribution are a major health hazard. These toxic emissions contribute to acid rain, smog and numerous other harmful effects associated with the use of petroleum, coal and natural gas. By clogging sewer pipes, plastic bags also create stagnant water; stagnant water produces the ideal habitat for mosquitoes, which have the potential to spread diseases, such as encephalitis, dengue fever and malaria.

The manufacture of plastic bags uses large quantities of non-renewable resources, especially petroleum.

If you care about your children's and grandchildren's futures, then you will say YES to banning plastic bags.

Emily Dunn

NO

Dear Sir/Madam,

The 'no plastic bags' lobby make a lot of noise and quote a lot of figures, but when you look at what they say closely, they are simply being hysterical!

Plastic bags represent only 0.1% of Australia's landfill waste. In terms of Australia's total waste plastics problem, plastic bags make a negligible contribution. Approximately 6.9 billion bags are currently consumed in Australia per year – equivalent to over 37 tonnes of polymer. However, 37 tonnes of polymer is equivalent to only 2.5% of total plastics consumed in Australia per year.

Many plastic shopping bags are used beyond their 'single use' life. They are reused as waste bags or bin liners, lunch bags and general carry bags. It is estimated that approximately 60% of the bags taken home are reused.

The current plastic shopping bag is cheap, lightweight, functional, moisture-resistant, allows for quick packing at the supermarket and is very strong for its weight. Plastic bags perform an important task in product and food safety, keeping uncooked meat or cleaning products separate from other foods.

Plastic bags have environmental advantages. Plastic bags help contain other forms of litter and prevent it leaching out and polluting the soil and contaminating the water table. For example, organic matter such as food waste emits tonnes of greenhouse gases when degrading. Containing this waste in plastic bags may protect the environment.

Alternatives to plastic bags cause environmental harm. A cotton bag is made from a crop that is the most expensive fibre grown in terms of water use, pesticide and energy input. The 'green' bags, which are made from non-woven polypropylene, are designed to have a relatively long life but they are not designed to break down. Polypropylene is a byproduct of oil refining, so not only is it not biodegradable, but it adds to the depletion of fossil fuels and the creation of greenhouse gases.

You want facts? You've got facts. Now, get on with life and enjoy the convenience, versatility and safety a plastic bag offers you.

John Keating

9780170462860

Year 9 Literacy

Reading Test 1

Writing time: 65 minutes

Use 2B pencil only

Instructions

- Write your **student name** in the space provided.
- You must be silent during the test.
- If you need to speak to the teacher, raise your hand. Do not speak to other students.
- Answer all questions using a 2B pencil.
- If you wish to change your answer, erase it very thoroughly and then write your new answer.

Student name:

Text 1: *Animal Talk* Questions

Shade one box to show the correct answer to the following questions.

1 Animals communicate through

SHADE ONE BOX

- ☐ complex games.
- ☐ simple drawings.
- ☐ sounds and gestures.
- ☐ mimicking our words.

2 It seems the most complex animal communication occurs among

SHADE ONE BOX

- ☐ cats.
- ☐ insects.
- ☐ birds.
- ☐ sea creatures.

3 The creature that probably has the most complex forms of communication is the

SHADE ONE BOX

- ☐ bee.
- ☐ dog.
- ☐ whale.
- ☐ dinosaur.

4 Cuttlefish communicate with several other cuttlefish at a time by

SHADE ONE BOX

- ☐ singing.
- ☐ making patterns.
- ☐ dancing.
- ☐ making clicking sounds.

5 The best indicator of capacity for complex communication in animals seems to be

SHADE ONE BOX

- ☐ brain size.
- ☐ the size of the animal.
- ☐ sounds that sound like human words.
- ☐ the variety of types communication used.

9780170462860

Text 2: *Tung Ngo* Questions

Shade one box to show the correct answer to the following questions.

1 Tung Ngo came to Australia when he was

SHADE ONE BOX

- ☐ 11.
- ☐ 12.
- ☐ 21.
- ☐ 22.

2 Tung Ngo thinks of himself as

SHADE ONE BOX

- ☐ primarily Vietnamese.
- ☐ an ordinary Australian.
- ☐ confused about his identity.

3 Tung Ngo stood for the local council because

SHADE ONE BOX

- ☐ he wanted to become powerful.
- ☐ he wanted to impress the National Front.
- ☐ he wanted the Vietnamese community to like him.
- ☐ he wanted to know who the people actually supported.

4 According to Tung Ngo the most difficult thing he faced at school was

SHADE ONE BOX

- ☐ racism.
- ☐ ignorance.
- ☐ his appearance.
- ☐ the English language.

5 In saying he's involved in 'paying the bills' Tung Ngo means

SHADE ONE BOX

- ☐ he's repaying his outstanding debts.
- ☐ the Council is paying bills for people who can't pay them.
- ☐ he's giving back to the community that has given to him.
- ☐ he's paying some of the bills of the Vietnamese community.

6 Tung Ngo believes the best way to enjoy being a young Australian is to

SHADE ONE BOX

- ☐ stand for council.
- ☐ play cricket and footy.
- ☐ leave behind his Vietnamese culture.
- ☐ be open to other influences.

Text 3: *Fair Trade* Questions

Shade one box to show the correct answer to the following questions.

1 The fair trade movement began in

SHADE ONE BOX

☐ the 1970s.

☐ the 1960s.

☐ the 1950s.

☐ the 1940s.

2 Fair trade is a movement that is a response to

SHADE ONE BOX

☐ Oxfam.

☐ globalisation.

☐ poor farming methods.

☐ environmental destruction.

3 Fair traders work with local farmers to

SHADE ONE BOX

☐ sell their produce locally.

☐ sell local produce globally.

☐ produce cheap goods for tourists.

☐ bring global products into their local community.

4 A 'cup of joe' is

SHADE ONE BOX

☐ slang for a cup of coffee.

☐ an exotic drink from Honduras.

☐ figurative language for 'a cup of happiness'.

☐ any type of beverage sold under a fair trade agreement.

5 The stance taken in this piece on fair trade is generally

SHADE ONE BOX

☐ neutral.

☐ positive.

☐ negative.

☐ ambiguous.

6 Fair trade is mainly concerned about coffee and grain farmers. True or false?

WRITE YOUR OWN ANSWER

Use evidence from the text to support your answer.

____

____

____

9780170462860

Text 4: *Goha Gives His Son a Lesson* Questions

Shade one box to show the correct answer to the following questions.

1 Goha's son is unable to do anything because

SHADE ONE BOX

- ☐ he is afraid of donkeys.
- ☐ he is afraid of hurting himself.
- ☐ he doesn't want to embarrass his father.
- ☐ he is afraid other people will think he is silly.

2 Goha is shown to be

SHADE ONE BOX

- ☐ a wise man.
- ☐ a harsh father.
- ☐ a foolish man.
- ☐ someone who dislikes his neighbours.

3 In this story Goha is trying to show his son

SHADE ONE BOX

- ☐ how to make decisions.
- ☐ that donkeys are contrary animals.
- ☐ something about the nature of people.
- ☐ to respect the views of his neighbours.

4 The purpose of the story is

SHADE ONE BOX

- ☐ record a historic event.
- ☐ explore the strength of donkeys.
- ☐ to make a serious point in an amusing way.
- ☐ to explore transport options in Middle Eastern countries.

5 'This time Goha was at a loss.' This means Goha

SHADE ONE BOX

- ☐ regretted his wife's absence.
- ☐ had lost some of his valuables.
- ☐ couldn't find the correct road home.
- ☐ couldn't understand other people's thinking.

Text 5: *Preschool Teacher* Questions

Shade one box to show the correct answer to the following questions.

1 Becoming a preschool teacher was 'instinctive' for Kristin Cantwell. This means she felt

SHADE ONE BOX

- ☐ it was a natural choice.
- ☐ it was a difficult choice.
- ☐ it was not her first choice.
- ☐ it was the only choice available.

2 Kristin Cantwell has been a preschool teacher for

SHADE ONE BOX

- ☐ 18 years.
- ☐ 33 years.
- ☐ 40 years.
- ☐ 54 years.

3 According to the text, learning at preschool takes place

SHADE ONE BOX

- ☐ occasionally.
- ☐ through play.
- ☐ during formal lessons.
- ☐ for only part of each session.

4 One reason that Mrs Cantwell enjoys preschool children is because

SHADE ONE BOX

- ☐ they're cute.
- ☐ they're honest.
- ☐ they're easy to discipline.
- ☐ the preschool day is shorter than primary or secondary school.

5 The phrase 'begged, bullied and bribed' is an example of

SHADE ONE BOX

- ☐ metaphor.
- ☐ alliteration.
- ☐ exaggeration.
- ☐ figurative language.

6 According to the text the parents at Blue Hills Preschool don't want Kristin Cantwell to retire because

SHADE ONE BOX

- ☐ she is very patient with their children.
- ☐ they don't want to have to search for a new teacher.
- ☐ they think an older teacher is better than a younger teacher.
- ☐ they're worried the preschool might close if they don't find a suitable replacement.

9780170462860

Text 6: *Think Twice Before You Slam That Can!* Questions

Shade one box to show the correct answer to the following questions.

1 To rehydrate the body after intense exercise, a drink should contain the following

SHADE ONE BOX

- ☐ electrolytes.
- ☐ sugar and water.
- ☐ palatable flavouring.
- ☐ salts, carbohydrates and sugar.

2 Sport drinks should be consumed by

SHADE ONE BOX

- ☐ only elite athletes.
- ☐ students when exercising.
- ☐ everyone who exercises.
- ☐ people who require re-hydration after exercise.

3 If your body doesn't consume all the ingredients in sports drinks it will

SHADE ONE BOX

- ☐ turn them into fat.
- ☐ absorb them into tissue.
- ☐ pass them in your urine.
- ☐ store them for use next time you exercise.

4 Caffeine and guarana help you to

SHADE ONE BOX

- ☐ keep calm.
- ☐ sleep better.
- ☐ be more alert.
- ☐ be more co-ordinated.

5 This piece suggests that the main health risk associated with energy drinks is

SHADE ONE BOX

- ☐ stroke.
- ☐ tooth decay.
- ☐ weight gain.
- ☐ palpitations.

6 The best description of the view taken on sports and energy drinks in this article is

SHADE ONE BOX

- ☐ alarmist.
- ☐ against such drinks.
- ☐ cautious about the drinks.
- ☐ favourable toward such drinks.

Text 7: A *Mistake* Questions

Shade one box to show the correct answer to the following questions.

1 This poem is written in the

SHADE ONE BOX

- ☐ first person.
- ☐ second person.
- ☐ third person.

2 The mistake the speaker of the poem makes at age three or four is

SHADE ONE BOX

- ☐ she thought her brother was famous.
- ☐ she thought Elvis Presley came to her house.
- ☐ she hadn't behaved well when Elvis Presley visited.
- ☐ she thought Elvis Presley played the guitar but then discovered it was the ukulele.

3 The three dots at the end of the first stanza indicate

SHADE ONE BOX

- ☐ the writer has forgotten what was said.
- ☐ the rest of the conversation was boring.
- ☐ that the writer is unsure of how to proceed.
- ☐ the details of the conversation aren't important.

4 In the second stanza, the writer refers to 'my first quick click of readjustment'; 'quick click' is an example of

SHADE ONE BOX

- ☐ alliteration.
- ☐ exaggeration.
- ☐ onomatopoeia.
- ☐ personification.

5 This is a poem

SHADE ONE BOX

- ☐ about Elvis Presley visiting a family.
- ☐ about a boy who looked like Elvis Presley.
- ☐ that shows how silly our childhood perceptions can be.
- ☐ that challenges the idea that adult perceptions are always more accurate than a child's.

9780170462860

Text 8: *Should We Ban Plastic Bags?* Questions

Shade one box to show the correct answer to the following questions.

1 The tone of Emily's letter is

SHADE ONE BOX

- ☐ serious.
- ☐ emotive.
- ☐ flippant.
- ☐ inflammatory.

2 Emily's point of view is supported by

SHADE ONE BOX

- ☐ personal anecdotes.
- ☐ quotes from experts.
- ☐ statistics exclusively.
- ☐ scientific information.

3 Plastic bags are attractive to marine life because

SHADE ONE BOX

- ☐ they're colourful.
- ☐ they look like food.
- ☐ they like the taste of plastic.
- ☐ they can use them in their 'nests'.

4 According to John's letter, plastic bags make up

SHADE ONE BOX

- ☐ 0.01% of landfill.
- ☐ 0.1% of landfill.
- ☐ 2.5% of landfill.
- ☐ 6.9% of landfill.

5 Plastic bags are re-used in

SHADE ONE BOX

- ☐ 25% of cases.
- ☐ 37% of cases.
- ☐ 60% of cases.
- ☐ 69% of cases.

6 The tone of the last paragraph of John's letter is best described as

SHADE ONE BOX

- ☐ jovial.
- ☐ neutral.
- ☐ exasperated.
- ☐ disinterested.

Year 9 Literacy

Writing Test 1

Writing time: 40 minutes

Use 2B pencil, blue or black pen only

Instructions

- Write your **student name** in the space provided.
- You must be silent during the test.
- If you need to speak to the teacher, raise your hand. Do not speak to other students.
- Use a pencil or a black or blue pen only.
- Use the lines provided. Do not write in the borders.

Student name:

Criteria:

There are ten criteria assessed in the writing task:

- audience
- text structure
- characters
- events
- vocabulary
- sentence structure
- paragraphs
- cohesion
- punctuation
- spelling.

Travel

You are going to write an expository text.

The idea for your story is 'travel'.

Your exposition might be an argumentative essay about the value of people travelling beyond their usual environment or homes to other places.

It could be the text of a persuasive speech or public address to encourage time travel.

You could write a review of a holiday destination.

Think about

- the central argument you are making
- the logical, relevant points that support your argument
- the conclusion you will draw at the end of your argument.

Remember to

- write a plan for the text
- write in sentences
- look at your choice of words, spelling, punctuation and use of paragraphs
- check and edit your work when you have finished writing.

9780170462860

Writing Test 1 – Exposition

Look at the stimulus. Brainstorm your ideas and then use this box to write a clear plan. Allow no more than five minutes. This planning will not be marked.

Year 9 Literacy

Language Conventions Test 2

Writing time: 45 minutes

Use 2B pencil only

Instructions

- Write your **student name** in the space provided.
- You must be silent during the test.
- If you need to speak to the teacher, raise your hand. Do not speak to other students.
- Answer all questions using a 2B pencil.
- If you wish to change your answer, erase it very thoroughly and then write your new answer.

Student name:

WRITE YOUR OWN ANSWER

The spelling mistakes in these texts have been circled. Write the correct spelling for each circled word in the box provided.

1 The mayre of the city was given the task

of opening the oprah season. She arrived

dramatically in a helicopta.

WRITE YOUR OWN ANSWER

2 When we celebrate national days at our school

we invite the appropriate ambasador to attend.

They usually manage to fit us into their busy shedules.

In general they find such visits most plesurable.

WRITE YOUR OWN ANSWER

3 There are many ocupations to consider if you wish

to help people. The work an atturney does is varied

and of great importance in the community.

Each sentence has one word that is incorrect.
Write the correct spelling of the word in the box.

WRITE YOUR OWN ANSWER

4 Our appreciation of language is enriched when we know the origens of words.

5 It is best to use a local provider if you want promt delivery.

6 We watched the primary students play in order to recroot some of them into our team.

7 The rythms of South American music are very lively.

8 Lether is a long-wearing material if you care for it properly.

9 The enginear was called in to assess the safety of the bridge.

10 The students sent a delagation to speak to the deputy principal.

11 The flavour of dark chocolate is particularly intens.

9780170462860

WRITE YOUR OWN ANSWER

Each sentence has one word that is incorrect.
Write the correct spelling of the word in the box.

12 The controversie was reported in the daily papers.

13 It is so good to breath fresh mountain air.

14 When you study another language you also learn about cultueral aspects of countries.

15 You have to have the aproval of your parents or guardian to attend the camp.

16 In order to acess the school network you need a password.

17 A secret balot was held to elect the captain.

18 Circut training is an excellent way to develop different muscle groups.

19 Sereal is good to eat if you want a sustaining breakfast.

20 Which of the following correctly completes the sentence?

SHADE ONE BOX

Mia felt that she [ ] spent more time with her grandmother.

☐ should'ave ☐ should've ☐ should of ☐ shouldve

21 Which of the following correctly completes the sentence?

SHADE ONE BOX

Hamish has [ ] if it is possible to attend the concert with his friends.

☐ ask ☐ asked ☐ asks ☐ will ask

22 Which of the following correctly completes the sentence?

SHADE ONE BOX

David, [ ] likely to be chosen as the school's representative, is a very thoughtful person.

☐ who's ☐ whose' ☐ whos ☐ whose

23 Which of the following has the correct punctuation?

SHADE ONE BOX

☐ Golding says, 'thinking skills are at the very core of academic success'
☐ Golding says, 'Thinking skills are at the very core of academic success.'

☐ Golding says 'thinking skills are at the very core of academic success.'

☐ Golding says Thinking skills are at the very core of academic success.'

24 Which of the following correctly completes the sentence?

SHADE ONE BOX

Lily prefers to be known as ________ she calls a 'fashionista'.

☐ when ☐ who ☐ what ☐ why

25 Which of the following correctly completes the sentence?

SHADE ONE BOX

John ________ gladly driven the girls home if they had asked him.

☐ would of ☐ would've ☐ would ☐ would'ave

26 Shade one box to show where the missing apostrophe (') should go.

SHADE ONE BOX

The two buildings ☐ doors, ☐ windows ☐ and blinds ☐ were damaged in the blast.

27 Which of the following correctly completes the sentence?

SHADE ONE BOX

I could tell from the tone of her voice
that she was taking things ________ .

☐ really serious ☐ real serious ☐ really seriously ☐ real seriously

28 Which of the following has the correct punctuation?

SHADE ONE BOX

☐ Spain is a beautiful country; the beache's are warm, sandy and spotlessly clean.

☐ Spain is a beautiful country; the beaches are warm, sandy and spotlessly clean.

☐ Spain is a beautiful country, the beaches are warm, sandy and spotlessly clean.

☐ Spain is a beautiful country; the beaches are warm sandy and spotlessly clean.

29 Which of the following correctly completes the sentence?

SHADE ONE BOX

The hockey team played with an ________ commitment.

☐ fierce ☐ savage ☐ relentless ☐ intense

30 Which sentence has the correct punctuation?

SHADE ONE BOX

- [ ] 'The culprit' Nicky said, 'has never been found.'
- [ ] 'The culprit, Nicky said, has never been found.'
- [ ] 'The culprit,' Nicky said, 'has never been found.'
- [ ] 'The culprit,' Nicky said. 'Has never been found.'

31 Which sentence has the correct punctuation?

SHADE ONE BOX

- [ ] After stealing Anitas car, the thief lost his way and was apprehended by the police.
- [ ] After stealing Anita's car, the thief lost his way and was apprehended by the police.
- [ ] After stealing Anita's car the thief, lost his way. and was apprehended by the police.
- [ ] After stealing Anita's car the thief lost his way and was apprehended by the police

32 Which of the following correctly completes the sentence?

SHADE ONE BOX

The [ ] raw materials storerooms is in the next street.

- [ ] factorys
- [ ] factories
- [ ] factory's
- [ ] factorie's

33 Which sentence has the correct punctuation?

SHADE ONE BOX

- [ ] 'Well,' she said, 'you certainly didn't waste any time.'
- [ ] 'Well,' she said, 'You certainly didn't waste any time.'
- [ ] 'Well,' she said, 'you certainly didn't waste any time'.
- [ ] 'Well, she said, you certainly didn't waste any time.'

34 Which sentence has the correct punctuation?

SHADE ONE BOX

- [ ] The tennis coach said to try a different stroke, so I tried to hit a flat forehand.
- [ ] The tennis coach said, to try a different stroke so I tried to hit a flat forehand.
- [ ] The tennis coach said, 'to try a different stroke. So I tried to hit a flat forehand'
- [ ] The tennis coach said, 'To try a different stroke, so I tried to hit a flat forehand.'

35 Which sentence has the correct punctuation?

SHADE ONE BOX

- [ ] My favorite teacher, who happens to be my mothers best friend, is moving to a new school next term
- [ ] My favorite teacher, who happens to be my mother's best friend, is moving to a new school next term.

- [ ] My favorite teacher who happens to be my mothers best friend, is moving to a new school next term.
- [ ] My favorite teacher, who happens to be my mothers' best friend, is moving to a new school, next term.

36 Which sentence has the correct punctuation?

SHADE ONE BOX

- [ ] She always enjoyed: sweets, chocolate, marshmallows and nougat.
- [ ] She always enjoyed sweets, chocolate, marshmallows and nougat.
- [ ] She always enjoyed sweet's, chocolate, marshmallows and nougat.
- [ ] She always enjoyed sweets chocolate marshmallows and nougat.

Read the following text and answer the questions below.

The Australian Mist: Our Very Own Moggie

The Australian Mist is a breed developed in Australia from the cross-breeding of Burmese, Abyssinian and Australian domestic shorthair cats. It is a medium sized cat and is very people-oriented. The short coat has a pattern of spots or marbling against a darker background. The legs and tail are barred and the face is lined. Accepted colours include brown, blue, chocolate, lilac, gold and peach.

37 The text is written in the

SHADE ONE BOX

- [ ] past tense.
- [ ] present tense.
- [ ] future tense.

38 In this text the words Burmese and Abyssinian are capitalised because

SHADE ONE BOX

- [ ] they are not of Australian origin.
- [ ] the author wants to draw attention to them.
- [ ] they are proper nouns.
- [ ] they are difficult to pronounce.

9780170462860

Read the following text and answer the questions below.

Zines

A zine (pronounced 'zeen' and short for magazine or fanzine) is a self-published, not for profit periodical put out by someone who has some ideas or something to say, a copy machine, and a stapler.

Electronic zines (called E-Zines) have become extremely popular because of the ease of publication, the lack of associated printing costs and the potential for wide exposure. Most sites for E-Zines are accessible to millions of people, literally.

39 In the first sentence the word 'periodical' is used as

- ☐ a verb.
- ☐ a noun.
- ☐ an adjective.
- ☐ an adverb.

SHADE ONE BOX

40 This text has been written in the

- ☐ first person.
- ☐ second person.
- ☐ third person.

SHADE ONE BOX

41 In the final sentence the word 'literally' is used as

- ☐ a verb.
- ☐ a noun.
- ☐ an adjective.
- ☐ an adverb.

SHADE ONE BOX

Read the following text and answer the questions below.

Marvellous Mystical Machu Picchu

In the 15th century, the Incan Emperor Pachacútec built a city in the clouds on a mountain in the Peruvian Andes known as Machu Picchu ('old mountain'). It is situated at a height of 9060 feet, 2430 metres above sea-level. It is Peru's most famous tourist attraction and also a UN World Heritage site.

It was probably abandoned by the Incas because of a smallpox outbreak and, after the Spanish defeated the Incan Empire, the city remained 'lost' for over three centuries. It was rediscovered by Hiram Bingham in 1911.

42 In the first sentence, the words 'old mountain' are placed in inverted commas because

SHADE ONE BOX

- ☐ they are a title.
- ☐ they are technical words.
- ☐ they are an actual quote.
- ☐ they are a translation from another language.

43 In the title, *Marvellous Mystical* is an example of

SHADE ONE BOX

- ☐ a rhyme.
- ☐ a simile.
- ☐ alliteration.
- ☐ exaggeration.

44 In the second last sentence, the word 'Incan' is used as

SHADE ONE BOX

- ☐ a verb.
- ☐ a noun.
- ☐ an adjective.
- ☐ an adverb.

9780170462860

Year 9 Literacy

Reading Magazine 2

Meeting People Online

It is not uncommon to want to explore the internet and start friendships online with people you may not have met face-to-face. You can form rewarding and lifelong friendships this way, as well as connect with people you may not otherwise find it easy to meet in real life due to geographical distance.

You might meet people online through forums, chatrooms, or online social networks such as Myspace or Facebook.

There are, however, a few things you should remember to meet people safely online and avoid undesirable situations:

- Be careful in chat rooms. Even though someone might say they're a young person, there's no way of really knowing this is the case.
- On social networking sites such as Myspace and Facebook keep your profile private if possible, and only befriend people known to you.
- Never give out personal details such as your home address, phone number, school, university or workplace to anybody you don't know online (or where it could be seen publicly by people you don't know).
- Never arrange to meet anyone unless someone goes with you and you meet in a public place. People you contact online are not always who they seem or who they say they are.

If you are being bullied online by people you meet there, tell someone you trust about it.

9780170462860

Chocolate

Heather Catchpole

Chocolate is a mixture of sugar, fat and cocoa. Cocoa is a brown powder that's made from the Cacao bean. This amazing bean grows on trees in countries around the equator (the imaginary line around the centre of the Earth).

The first chocolate was made by ancient South American civilisations thousands of years ago, by either the Mayan, or the Olmec civilisation. They ground Cacao beans into powder and mixed it with water, wine, spices and even chilli. Phew! Talk about hot chocolate!

Before sugar is added, chocolate is very bitter. But adding sugar and fats such as cocoa butter, which is the fat found naturally in cocoa beans, makes chocolate very hard to resist.

Why is chocolate good to eat? Scientists that study chocolates have found that despite many people experiencing chocolate cravings, chocolate isn't really addictive. It does contain some chemicals that stimulate the brain, making you feel more alert. Caffeine is a drug found in coffee and some soft drinks that increases your heart rate. Although chocolate doesn't contain caffeine, it contains chemicals that have a similar effect.

Some scientists think chocolate also contains feel-good chemicals that trick the brain into thinking it has to make chemicals that make you feel relaxed and pleasurable. So chocolate might perk you up and soothe you at the same time.

Is chocolate bad for you? The good news is that chocolate is no worse for your body than anything else that is sweet, although all sweet foods contain sugar, which among other things can cause tooth decay.

Cocoa might even be good for you. Cocoa contains chemicals called phenols, which are antioxidants. Antioxidants neutralise chemicals in your body that attack other chemicals and increase the chances of getting heart disease.

Like everything else, chocolate should be eaten in moderation. So don't get too carried away around Easter time.

Anzac Memories

Inga Clendinner

In the late 1930s, when I was still too young to count as female (women were of course banned from this sacred men's business), my father used to smuggle me into the Dawn Service at Johnstone's Park in Geelong. My father had not been at Gallipoli, but he had been on the Western Front. I had only the vaguest notion of the history – I knew that there had been a battle, and that we had lost – but I felt and still feel the emotions of the men standing silently around me. One of my few relics is a buff-coloured card from my father's furniture manufactory. It has 'From Bench to You' printed on one side, with the factory's address and telephone number, and on the other, in my father's elegant upright hand, this. He must have been going to read it at the Dawn Service:

Now let us praise famous men, and our fathers that begat us. There be of them that have left a name behind them, that their praises might be reported. And some there be which have no memorial, who are perished as tho' they had never been born, but their glory shall not be blotted out. Their bodies are buried in peace and their name liveth for evermore.

My throat still tightens as I read those words. The sound of a lone bugle, the murmur of magpies in a grey dawn, sweep me back into that strange blend of emotions – pride, grief, anger – as if it were yesterday.

 9780170462860

Bird Strikes Common Risk for Aircraft

Jennifer Viegas

The location of an airport and quieter airplane engines could increase the chances of bird-air strikes, say US federal aviation officials.

The admission comes days after US Airways flight 1549 is believed to have collided with a flock of geese seconds after takeoff from LaGuardia airport on 15 January. All 155 passengers and crew survived Thursday's event, due in part to the skilful manoeuvring of the pilot.

However, the emergency water landing highlights at least three risk factors for bird-air strikes that may receive more attention in the future.

Questions that may be asked include: Do flight paths at particular airports cross with bird migratory paths? Can improved technologies prevent birds from being sucked into engines? Does the airport have a trained biologist present to help mitigate the problem?

'If you look outside your plane window before takeoff and see an individual in a vehicle scanning the runway, there's a good chance he's a biologist monitoring the airport for birds', says US Department of Agriculture spokesman Larry Hawkins.

Hawkins is a member of the federal government's Animal and Plant Health Inspection Service, which performs assessment management plans for airports that then have the option of contracting with them to bring in a biologist and support staff...

...'Our prevention tactics include habitat modification, removal of wildlife, if necessary, and hazing', he says, explaining that hazing can involve everything from setting up brightly coloured scarecrow-type balloons that frighten birds to audible scaring...

In the flight path

An airport's location can also increase the chances of a bird strike, Hawkins suggests, with airports near water being at greater risk, along with airports that intersect 'bird flyways'.

'These are flight paths followed by migrating birds,' he explains. 'Some California airports, for example, cross the Pacific Flyway.'

Planes are at greatest risk for a bird strike during takeoffs and landings, since above this 'risk zone' they fly higher than birds...

'Feathered bullets'

Dale Oderman, an associate professor of aviation technology at Purdue University, says that birds sometimes get near a plane engine's intake, which consists of multiple compressor blades. If the bird impact leads to a blade breaking, it can turn a blade into a dangerous piece of shrapnel, potentially causing other damage.

Both Hawkins and Oderman agree that even smaller birds, such as starlings, can damage planes, especially if the aircraft collides with a flock.

Bird Strike Committee USA even refers to starlings as 'feathered bullets', since they say these birds possess 'a body density 27 per cent higher than herring gulls'.

Better technologies are being sought to make plane engines less vulnerable to bird air strikes, but airplane improvements ironically may now be increasing avian-aviator collisions.

'Fan jets are quieter and more efficient,' Hawkins says, 'but birds can't hear them as well, so the planes themselves are less of a deterrent.'

9780170462860

Vanishing Species

Jennifer Strauss

The child
(computer games abandoned)
comes tidily to breakfast
on coffee and croissants.
'I didn't'
she declares, 'much care
for last night's sitter.
She talked too much.
She wouldn't
let me play my video;
she didn't read from a book
she talked a story.
It was weird –
there was this naughty mother
sent her little girl out
all by herself, into the woods.'
The foundations
of order being shaken
a muscle quivers
in the mock-adult face
'Daddy,' she says
'What are woods?
What's a wolf?
What's a riding hood?
What's a red?'

Banknote Technology

Australia leads the world in plastic banknote technology.

What's the problem?

Paper banknotes wear out quickly, particularly if they get wet. They are also fairly easy to counterfeit – despite security measures, such as watermarks and having metallic threads within the notes. The emergence of colour photocopiers and scanners has made it easier to reproduce paper money.

A great Aussie solution

CSIRO and Note Printing Australia (part of the Reserve Bank of Australia) developed polymer money. The world's first polymer banknote was the $10 commemorative note issued in January 1988 to mark the Australian Bicentenary. By 1996, all Australians were using plastic money, and that doesn't mean whipping out their credit cards! The new bills are much more durable and have proven a challenge for counterfeiters.

How does it work?

Australia's plastic money is made of a non-porous polymer with a specially developed protective coating so the notes stay cleaner and don't absorb moisture. They last on average four to five times longer in circulation, with the plastic $5 note lasting for around 40 months, compared to six months for the paper $5. After it does wear out, polymer money is recycled into plastic products such as compost bins and plumbing fittings.

The polymer substrate behaves a lot like paper and conventional printing techniques are used to apply ink to the surface. The major security measure is a see-through window which makes the plastic money difficult to reproduce using photocopiers and scanners.

The future

Australia was the first country to have all polymer banknotes, but the rest of the world is starting to follow our lead. Note Printing Australia has produced banknotes for Thailand, Indonesia, Papua New Guinea, Kuwait, Western Samoa, Singapore, Brunei, Sri Lanka and New Zealand.

Cloning

YES

Dear Sir/ Madam,

I recently lost my beloved Cavalier King Charles Spaniel, Hamish. He was the best dog that ever walked the earth. If cloning had been legal I could now be enjoying Hamish all over again. Why do selfish people want to take away my happiness?

But it's not just my happiness I'm concerned about. If cloning was made legal we could create a human repair kit. People could have their own organs cloned and have them ready to replace the originals when the need arises. We wouldn't need to worry about rates of organ donation and the problem of donor organ rejection would be solved for ever.

If we had cloning we would be able to save endangered animals. It's not the animals that have made themselves endangered! It's us – the human race. If we have the technology to clone animals – and Dolly the sheep proves we do – then the least we can do is bring them back from the brink – which we have created.

And those people who say cloning isn't 'natural' should go back to school and learn some more biology. Cloning already occurs 'naturally' in some animals such as insects and frogs in a process called *parthenogenesis*. This is where an egg develops without fertilisation.

People who don't like cloning don't have to use it. They shouldn't be allowed, however, to stop those of us who do.

Yours

Sophie Harper

NO

Dear Sir/Madam,

I am writing to urge the community to think carefully before voting to allow cloning.

Just because we can, does it mean we should? I can buy a gun and shoot a person, but does that mean I should? Does it make it right just because I can do it? We really have to think about what we value and consider if cloning will take us in the opposite direction.

Even if cloning could be defended on moral grounds, it's currently a very imperfect technology. A very large percentage of cloning efforts end in failure. For example, it took 277 attempts to clone Dolly the sheep. And it has been seen in clones that have survived, that they have genetic problems that end in death. All this money gives us nothing that improves the daily lives of ordinary people.

Genetic diversity helps provide the pool of variations available for a robust human population. It is common knowledge that inbreeding animals can result in reduced variations and an increased risk of genetic defects. An example is hip dysplasia in pure-bred dogs. Mixed breeds tend to be more adaptable and healthier.

Finally, think of the psychological harm that cloning would inflict on a child. The cloned child would have no sense of individuality and uniqueness. Let's face it: cloning is a slippery slope to destruction.

Yours sincerely

Jorge Albertos

Some Chips With That?

Bernie Hobbs

If you're trying to diet away those winter love handles, you might want to think about hitting your fish and chip shop. Often and hard. But not to drown your cellulitic sorrows in tartare sauce – scientists in Western Australia reckon that eating a bit of fish each day helps improve your general health while you're living on carrot sticks and cottage cheese. It's the omega-3 fatty acids in the fish that do the trick. They're the good bits in some fats that help cut your blood pressure and cholesterol level – giving the old heart a bit of a break. But before you race off in your one-size-fits-all trackies to buy up enough fillets to see you through summer, you might want to think about the fish for a second. They've got a little problem of their own. Sure it's not in the league of your pokey-out thighs, but they're facing a little population crisis. Some kinds of shark, or beer-battered flake as we like to call them, are in pathetically low numbers. And gemfish are in so much strife that trawling them was outlawed a few years ago. Blue Fin Tuna are in huge danger of being fished out because they're worth a mint in Japan, and they're not as photogenic as dolphins. And the Orange Ruffie, which used to live in peace on the ocean floor, is now the most popular fish on American dinner plates. Add to that the enormous numbers of fish that are killed just because they were swimming with the wrong crowd when the trawler came through, and you get a feel for why 'eat more fish' isn't necessarily a good idea. So if it's omega-3 fatty acids you're after, why not do the fish a favour and get your good oil from another source – like flaxseed or canola. It'll cost you a trip to your local hippy emporium, but surely that's not too big a sacrifice to make for our scaly brothers and sisters.

9780170462860

Year 9 Literacy

Reading Test 2

Writing time: 65 minutes

Use 2B pencil only

Instructions

- Write **your name** in the space provided.
- You must be silent during the test.
- If you need to speak to the teacher, raise your hand. Do not speak to other students.
- Answer all questions using a 2B pencil.
- If you wish to change your answer, erase it very thoroughly and then write your new answer.

Student name:

Text 1: *Meeting People Online* Questions

Shade one box to show the correct answer to the following questions.

1 The writer of this piece suggests that one of the really good things about meeting people online is that

SHADE ONE BOX

- ☐ you can pretend to be someone else.
- ☐ you have time to think before writing.
- ☐ you can meet people from far-away places.
- ☐ you don't have to worry about your appearance.

2 The main reason the writer suggests it's important to be careful in chat rooms is because

SHADE ONE BOX

- ☐ they are monitored by authorities.
- ☐ you don't really know who you're talking to.
- ☐ people will judge you on the quality of your writing.
- ☐ someone might try to get you involved in illegal activities.

3 If you are going to meet an online friend in real life you should

SHADE ONE BOX

- ☐ notify the police.
- ☐ take someone with you.
- ☐ conceal your true identity
- ☐ arrange to meet in a private place.

4 If people are bullying you online you should

SHADE ONE BOX

- ☐ bully them back.
- ☐ just accept it and it might stop.
- ☐ arrange to meet them to discuss the problem.
- ☐ ask for guidance from someone you trust.

Text 2: *Chocolate* Questions

Shade one box to show the correct answer to the following questions.

1 Chocolate was first made by people in

SHADE ONE BOX

- ☐ Canada.
- ☐ North America.
- ☐ South America.
- ☐ Central America.

2 'Talk about hot chocolate!' This part of the text refers to

☐ ingredients in the hot chocolate.

☐ heating the hot chocolate.

☐ flavours of hot chocolate.

☐ discussions about hot chocolate.

SHADE ONE BOX

3 The writer suggests that one of the reasons chocolate is good to eat apart from the taste is

☐ it puts you to sleep.

☐ it acts as a brain stimulant.

☐ you can consume it as a solid or a liquid.

☐ you can combine it with lots of other flavours.

SHADE ONE BOX

4 According to the text, antioxidants in the body

☐ destroy phenols.

☐ increase your heart rate.

☐ create a feeling of well-being.

☐ cancel out dangerous chemicals.

SHADE ONE BOX

5 Chocolate should be eaten in moderation because

☐ it is addictive.

☐ it is expensive.

☐ it contains sugar.

☐ it contains caffeine.

SHADE ONE BOX

Text 3: *Anzac Memories* Questions

Shade one box to show the correct answer to the following questions.

1 The writer suggests that in the late 1930s gender roles were

☐ unclear.

☐ ridiculous.

☐ unimportant.

☐ clearly defined.

SHADE ONE BOX

2 The word 'smuggle' suggests the writer's attendance at the service

☐ was illegal.

☐ was thought to be inappropriate.

☐ would be laughed at.

☐ was an embarrassment to her father.

SHADE ONE BOX

3 The service, as presented from the child's perspective is

SHADE ONE BOX

☐ funny.

☐ boring.

☐ intense.

☐ depressing.

4 The piece that the writer's father was going to read at the service suggests

SHADE ONE BOX

☐ those who were not famous but sacrificed their lives should always be honoured.

☐ our fathers should not send us to war.

☐ war is something that should be forgotten.

☐ the sacrifice of a famous person is more valuable than that of an unknown person.

5 The writer's throat still 'tightens' as she reads those words because

SHADE ONE BOX

☐ the words anger her.

☐ she thinks war is pointless.

☐ they remind her of her father.

☐ she is moved by the sacrifice of human life in war.

Text 4: *Bird Strikes Common Risk for Aircraft* Questions

Shade one box to show the correct answer to the following questions.

1 The likelihood of bird strikes with aircraft could be due to

SHADE ONE BOX

☐ the time of the day.

☐ the colour of the aircraft.

☐ the location of an airport.

☐ the musical sound produced by some engines.

2 'Hazing' birds involves

SHADE ONE BOX

☐ shooting them with feather bullets.

☐ carefully removing the birds' nests.

☐ using vision and sound to scare them.

☐ spraying them with liquids they find offensive.

3 To minimise bird strikes airports should be located

SHADE ONE BOX

☐ close to water.

☐ away from trees.

☐ close to nearby cities.

☐ as far away from water as possible.

4 Planes are at greatest risk

SHADE ONE BOX

- [ ] whilst cruising at altitude.
- [ ] during take-off and landing.
- [ ] when taxiing to the runway.
- [ ] whilst waiting for the green light to take off.

5 Planes contribute to the problem of bird strike because

SHADE ONE BOX

- [ ] nowadays their engines are quieter.
- [ ] they are painted in colours that attract birds.
- [ ] they have nooks and crannies where birds can seek refuge and rest.
- [ ] they are too cumbersome to move away from flocks of birds quickly.

Text 5: *Vanishing Species* Questions

Shade one box to show the correct answer to the following questions.

1 The use of the word 'abandoned' suggests that

SHADE ONE BOX

- [ ] the child is spoilt and careless.
- [ ] the child is tired of playing computer games.
- [ ] the child has a bad temper when losing a game.
- [ ] the child doesn't know how to close down the computer.

2 The tone in which the child first speaks, 'I didn't much care…' is best described as

SHADE ONE BOX

- [ ] superior.
- [ ] respectful.
- [ ] distressed.
- [ ] compassionate.

3 The poet chooses to mention a breakfast of 'coffee and croissants'

SHADE ONE BOX

- [ ] to show how sophisticated the child is.
- [ ] to endorse this as a good breakfast for children.
- [ ] to show how well the parents care for their child.
- [ ] to make a comment about the social class from which the child comes.

4 The four questions at the end of the poem suggest

SHADE ONE BOX

- [ ] the child is not very intelligent.
- [ ] the child's vocabulary is severely limited.
- [ ] the child doesn't care for silly fairy stories.
- [ ] the child has missed out on some common childhood experience.

5 The title of the poem, 'Vanishing Species', refers to the poet's sense that

SHADE ONE BOX

- ☐ babysitters are increasingly rare.
- ☐ traditional children's stories are no longer valued.
- ☐ 'woods' are being razed at an alarming rate.
- ☐ parents are spending less time with their children.

Text 6: *Banknote Technology* Questions

Shade one box to show the correct answer to the following questions.

1 The first country to use all polymer banknotes was

SHADE ONE BOX

- ☐ Indonesia.
- ☐ Australia.
- ☐ Singapore.
- ☐ New Zealand.

2 One of the biggest problems with paper banknotes is

SHADE ONE BOX

- ☐ they are easy to copy.
- ☐ they stick together easily.
- ☐ they feel like other bits of paper.
- ☐ the colour range available is limited.

3 The world's first polymer banknote was

SHADE ONE BOX

- ☐ the $2 bill.
- ☐ the $5 bill.
- ☐ the $10 bill.
- ☐ the $20 bill.

4 The first polymer Australian banknote was issued to

SHADE ONE BOX

- ☐ commemorate the Australian Bicentenary.
- ☐ demonstrate international innovation.
- ☐ commemorate Australia Day, 1988.
- ☐ celebrate the founding of The Reserve Bank of Australia.

5 Compared to the paper $5 note, the plastic $5 note lasts an extra

SHADE ONE BOX

- ☐ 32 months.
- ☐ 34 months.
- ☐ 36 months.
- ☐ 38 months.

6 The feature that makes the polymer note more secure is

SHADE ONE BOX

- ☐ a watermark.
- ☐ metallic threads.
- ☐ a see-through window.
- ☐ a special ingredient in the plastic coating.

Text 7: *Cloning* Questions

Shade one box to show the correct answer to the following questions.

1 Sophie has written her letter in favour of cloning primarily because of

SHADE ONE BOX

- ☐ personal loss of a beloved pet.
- ☐ what she has recently learned in her biology class.
- ☐ she wants to be able to do what she thinks is right.
- ☐ she knows someone who needs a replacement organ.

2 Jorge has written his letter against cloning primarily because

SHADE ONE BOX

- ☐ he thinks cloning is a waste of money.
- ☐ he is worried about losing genetic diversity.
- ☐ he thinks it often doesn't work and therefore is a waste of time.
- ☐ he thinks the moral dimensions haven't been adequately explored.

3 Sophie believes that people who are against cloning are

SHADE ONE BOX

- ☐ stupid.
- ☐ selfish.
- ☐ unaware.
- ☐ stubborn.

4 Jorge believes that people who favour cloning are

SHADE ONE BOX

- ☐ selfish.
- ☐ stupid.
- ☐ greedy.
- ☐ thoughtless.

5 Parthenogenesis is a biological process where

SHADE ONE BOX

- ☐ twins are created.
- ☐ reproduction requires fertilisation.
- ☐ the egg is destroyed in the womb.
- ☐ reproduction occurs without fertilisation.

6 According to Jorge, genetic diversity is desirable because

SHADE ONE BOX

- [ ] lack of diversity is boring.
- [ ] it guards against genetic defects.
- [ ] it makes mixed breed animals popular.
- [ ] it helps people be more accepting of difference.

7 Which of the following best describes the tone of Sophie's letter?

SHADE ONE BOX

- [ ] furious
- [ ] defeated
- [ ] distressed
- [ ] aggressive

8 Which of the following best describes the tone of Jorge's letter?

SHADE ONE BOX

- [ ] angry
- [ ] pompous
- [ ] concerned
- [ ] dismissive

Text 8: *Some Chips With That?* Questions

Shade one box to show the correct answer to the following questions.

1 'Love handles' is a colloquial term for

SHADE ONE BOX

- [ ] fat deposited around the midriff.
- [ ] the shoulder blades on a person's back.
- [ ] the affectionate way two people hold hands.
- [ ] the spots where a person places their hands when hugging another.

2 Fish is good for your health because

SHADE ONE BOX

- [ ] it is white flesh.
- [ ] it is easier to digest than meat.
- [ ] it contains omega-3 fatty acids.
- [ ] the ocean is not as polluted as the land.

3 The fish population is under stress because of

SHADE ONE BOX

- [ ] pollution.
- [ ] over-fishing.
- [ ] lack of suitable food.
- [ ] an increase in the predator population.

9780170462860

4 Dolphins are not being 'fished out' because

SHADE ONE BOX

- [ ] they are too large.
- [ ] their flesh is not tasty.
- [ ] they appeal to humans.
- [ ] they are smart enough to get away.

5 You can find an alternative source of omega-3 fatty acids in

SHADE ONE BOX

- [ ] butter.
- [ ] chicken.
- [ ] lean red meat.
- [ ] canola oil.

6 This piece is about

SHADE ONE BOX

- [ ] omega-3 fatty acids.
- [ ] the need to preserve and protect our fish.
- [ ] strategies for losing weight.
- [ ] the importance of fish in our diet.

7 The tone of this piece is best described as

SHADE ONE BOX

- [ ] serious.
- [ ] conversational.
- [ ] indifferent.
- [ ] haranguing.

Year 9 Literacy

Writing Test 2

Writing time: 40 minutes

Use 2B pencil, blue or black pen only

Instructions

- Write your **student name** in the space provided.
- You must be silent during the test.
- If you need to speak to the teacher, raise your hand. Do not speak to other students.
- Use a pencil or a black or blue pen only.
- Use the lines provided. Do not write in the borders.

Student name:

Criteria:

There are ten criteria assessed in the writing task:

- audience
- text structure
- characters
- events
- vocabulary
- sentence structure
- paragraphs
- cohesion
- punctuation
- spelling.

Water

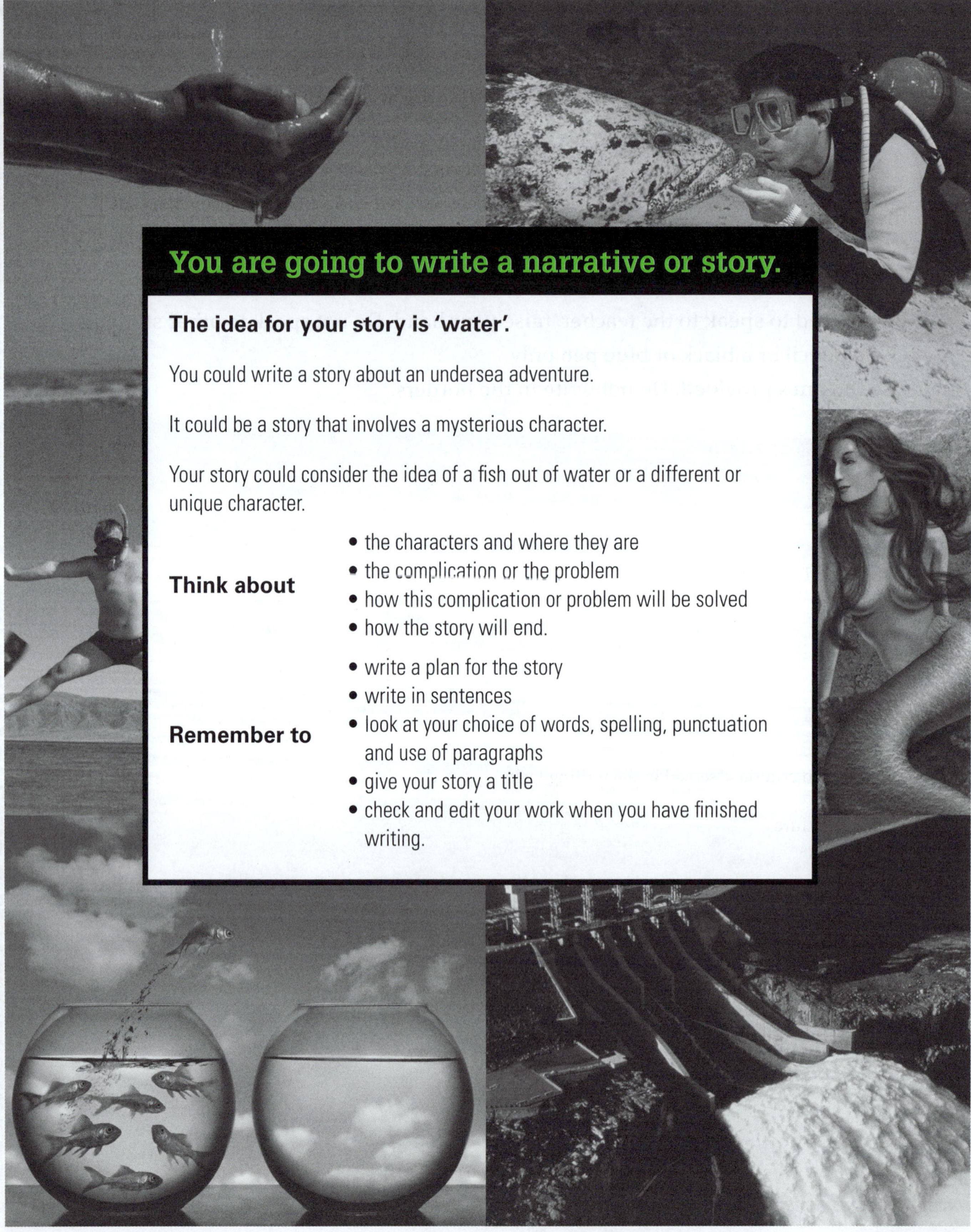

You are going to write a narrative or story.

The idea for your story is 'water'.

You could write a story about an undersea adventure.

It could be a story that involves a mysterious character.

Your story could consider the idea of a fish out of water or a different or unique character.

Think about

- the characters and where they are
- the complication or the problem
- how this complication or problem will be solved
- how the story will end.

Remember to

- write a plan for the story
- write in sentences
- look at your choice of words, spelling, punctuation and use of paragraphs
- give your story a title
- check and edit your work when you have finished writing.

Writing Test 2 – Narrative

Look at the stimulus. Brainstorm your ideas and then use this box to write a clear plan. Allow no more than five minutes. This planning will not be marked.

9780170462860

Glossary of Key Terms

Adjective
A word which modifies (adds more meaning) to a noun or a pronoun.
Adverb
A word which modifies (adds more meaning) to a verb, an adverb or an adjective.
Alliteration
A sound device where the consonant sound at the beginning of a word is repeated a number of times in a sequence of words; for example, 'big, bright and beautiful'. In this instance, alliteration occurs using the letter 'b'.
Apostrophe
A punctuation symbol (') used to indicate a contraction or possession. For example, don't is short for 'do not'. Another example is Alex's boots. The apostrophe in Alex's shows that the boots belong to Alex, indicating possession.
Climax
The pivotal point in a narrative (i.e. the most important or exciting event).
Cohesion
Describes the different language devices used to link words and sentences in a text smoothly and effectively to create meaning.
Comma
A punctuation symbol (,) used to indicate where a break might appear in a sentence. Commas may appear around a phrase or before a connecting word and the second part of a sentence. A comma can also be used to separate items in a list.
Complex sentence
Consists of one independent clause, and one or more dependent clauses. Commas are used to separate sentence clauses.
Composer
The original creator of a text.
Conjunctions
Words like 'and', 'but', 'when', 'or', etc., which connects sentences, phrases or clauses.
Context
Background information that helps us to understand the text; for example, who is writing it, who is the intended audience, why are they writing it?
Controlling idea
The main argument or purpose for writing as stated in the introduction.
Convention
A rule, method or practice established by usage or custom.
Deconstructing text
Involves the close reading of texts by breaking them down into components.
Dialogue
A conversation between two or more people.
Exposition (writing)
Argues a point of view.
First person
'I' and 'me'. Text written in the first person is personal and informal, and should therefore not be used in formal writing.
Inference
A conclusion based on reasoning and evidence.
Informative (writing)
Non-fiction report or descriptive text.
Language techniques or devices
These are used to expand meaning. For example, you could add adjectives to a noun, add adverbs to verbs. Phrases, similes, metaphors, etc. are also great devices that can be used effectively to illustrate a text.
Metaphor
A type of figurative language where the writer uses an implied comparison to add further meaning. For example consider the metaphor, 'perfect storm for investment'. It is used to describe difficult financial circumstances rather than describe the weather, as the use of 'storm' adds potency to how difficult the circumstances are.
Narrative (writing)
The telling of a story.
Narrator
The person (named or unknown) who tells a story.
Personal pronouns
Are used to substitute the names of the people or things that perform actions.
Personification
A type of figurative language where an inanimate thing or object is given human qualities. For example, 'the tree's knobbly fingers reached out towards me'. In this example the tree's branches are described as human fingers.
Point of view
Describes the perspective or source of a piece of writing.
Pun
The use of a word, or words that are formed or sounded alike but have different meanings, often for humorous effect.
Punctuation
Includes commas, full stops, quotation marks, etc. Punctuation helps to make the meaning of a text clear and therefore helps you to read a text.
Purpose
The reason for writing a text.
Recount
The retelling of an event.
Resolution
The part of a story that brings some conclusion to the complications in a narrative.
Rhetorical question
A question that does not require an answer because the answer is stated or obvious.
Scanning
To quickly read or glance over.
Second person
'You'. The second person helps to create the sense that the writer is talking directly to you, so you feel engaged and involved in the text.
Sequencing
Positions events and things into a an order that is logical and that you can easily follow.
Simile
A type of figurative language where the writer compares two things using 'like', 'as' or 'than'.
Skimming
To read, study, consider, etc., something in a surface or basic way.
Structure
The way a text is assembled or put together.

Symbol or motif

An object that represents something other than itself. Symbols or motifs may be used in writing as metaphors or repeated for cohesion.

Syntax

The way words are arranged in a sentence.

Tense

Is established through the verbs to specify whether an action happened in the past, present, future.

Thesis

The main argument or purpose for writing as stated in the introduction.

Third person

'He', 'she', 'it' and 'they'. The third person is more authoritative and objective than the first person ('I', 'me') or second person ('you').

Topic sentence

The first sentence of a paragraph that indicates what topic will be explored.

9780170462860